AF662695

Last Among Equals

Praise for *Last Among Equals*

'*Last Among Equals* mirrors the extraordinary perspicacity and complexity of village politics, seen through the lens of Bihar Manrega Watch, and is a counterpoint to the larger political discourse. M.R. Sharan holds the narrative together with sensitivity and deep understanding, tracing the journeys of remarkable human beings not born to privilege. It tells us that people, not statistics and theory, shape power and caste politics. This excellent book is invaluable reading for everyone bothered by inequality and injustice.' – **Aruna Roy**, Activist and Founder-member of the MKSS, NCPRI and SFD

'A fascinating personal odyssey and the trajectory of an underdeveloped state (Bihar), insiders and outsiders, effecting and impeding social change, the hideous hierarchy of caste and its frustratingly resolute persistence, the abuse of power and mechanisms to limit it: in *Last Among Equals*, M.R. Sharan boldly attempts all of these, combining the rigour of an academic with the engaging passion of a grounded citizen. And he succeeds.' – **Arvind Subramanian**, Former Chief Economic Advisor, Government of India

'How do people come together to claim their rights? How do they voice their aspirations, articulate their grievances? What builds solidarity? What must a person leave behind to lead such a movement? With a clear eye for detail and a riveting style, M.R. Sharan tells a story of mukhiyas and mazdoors, of dominant insiders and the marginalised, of a constitutional amendment as it takes shape on the ground, and of what sparks social change. In narrating the story of the people's movement of Muzaffarpur, he brings together the individual characters, the words, and the "feeling" of what he saw: a movement inspired by what Albert Hirschman might have called the "passion for what is possible". A fascinating read for anyone who cares about India.' – **Uma Mahadevan-Dasgupta**, Civil Servant

'This brilliant and insightful book helps us understand how local politics and citizen activism work in rural Bihar to influence people's lives. It interweaves two narratives–Sharan's own, drawn from many years of field research, and that of his friend, the remarkable young activist Sanjay Sahni, to show us how development economics can be considerably enriched when it is deeply engaged with the field.' – **Vijayendra Rao**, Lead Economist, Development Research Group, World Bank

'He succeeds brilliantly, bringing the reader a powerful cocktail of RCTs (randomised controlled trials) and Srilal Shukla's Raag Darbari. The writing is witty and poignant, the scholarship is deep, and the style is eminently readable.' – **Amit Basole, *The Hindu***

'Dr Sharan's narrative is deceptively easy to read. He is able to strike a fine balance between a personal story and a macrophenomenon. Moving away from frameworks and jargon to storytelling is not an easy transition for an academic. Dr Sharan does that without much compromise.' – **M.S. Sriram, *Business Standard***

'[A] masterclass on the Mahatma Gandhi National Rural Employment Act for the layperson. Throughout the book, Sharan attempts at bifurcating the narrative between "insiders" and "outsiders" in the realm of Bihar's caste politics.' – **Aaliya Waziri, *The Telegraph***

'Sharan's love for Bihar and its people shines through brightly. The book—which is an interesting mix of reportage, travelogue, commentary and analysis—is a must read for those interested in understanding the heady collision of economics, power and caste in rural India.' – **B. Baskar, *The Hindu BusinessLine***

'It is rare to read a book about the ground realities of something as messy as village politics in Bihar and leaves one with that elusive emotion: hope. And yet hope is inevitably what one is left with after reading this book. Hope that bottom-up citizens' movements can make a difference ... Hope that laws and accountability mechanisms are not just ideas on paper ... Hope that empirical development economics is not solely the pursuit of datasets and conducting surveys, but can actually be driven by big ideas. Hope that social science researchers are not just distant, objective observers of social systems ...' – **Rohit Chandra, *The India Forum***

'Sharan achieves what I would have thought was impossible: he narrates each of these stories with an adroit mixture of dispassionate analysis and passionate involvement, all of it backed up by minute observations. The word "ethnography" doesn't come up once in the entire book, but if you are a student wondering what the word means, this book is a very good introductory answer.' – **Ashish Kulkarni, *EconForEverybody.com***

Last Among Equals

Power, Caste & Politics in Bihar's Villages

M.R. SHARAN

First published by Context, an imprint of Westland Publications Private Limited, in 2021

Published by Context, an imprint of Westland Books, a division of Nasadiya Technologies Private Limited, in 2022

No. 269/2B, First Floor, 'Irai Arul', Vimalraj Street, Nethaji Nagar, Allappakkam Main Road, Maduravoyal, Chennai 600095

Westland, the Westland logo, Context and the Context logo are the trademarks of Nasadiya Technologies Private Limited, or its affiliates.

Copyright © M.R. Sharan, 2021

M.R. Sharan asserts the moral right to be identified as the author of this work.

ISBN: 9789395073165

10 9 8 7 6 5 4 3 2 1

The views and opinions expressed in this work are the author's own and the facts are as reported by him, and the publisher is in no way liable for the same.

All rights reserved

Typeset in Goudy Old Style by SÜRYA, New Delhi

Printed at Manipal Technologies Limited, Manipal

No part of this book may be reproduced, or stored in a retrieval system, or transmitted in any form or by any means, electronic, mechanical, photocopying, recording, or otherwise, without express written permission of the publisher.

For Apurva

'We are all born of the same source, a woman's womb ...
Is there anyone in this world who is born through the ears?'

– Basavanna, twelfth-century Bhakti poet

Contents

Introduction

When Mahatma Gandhi stated that India lived in its villages, he was reminding his audience, college-going elite youth, that most of India did not live like them.[1] Bihar—home to one in ten Indians, most of them deeply political—still largely lives in its villages. In 1917, Gandhi led the peasants and farmers of Champaran on the first Satyagraha against the colonial government in India. Nearly a hundred years later, in a village a hundred kilometres from Champaran, a group of workers—mazdoors—organised a peaceful protest meeting of their own against their local government. With the monsoons receding and sowing done, the mazdoors wanted work. They turned to their local officials, applying for work under the National Rural Employment Guarantee Act (NREGA). The NREGA is an India-wide rural work-on-demand scheme: mazdoors are to be provided work in their villages within fifteen days of applying.

With over a month having passed and no response, the mazdoors had called for a meeting and, in the spirit of Gandhian deliberation, also invited local government officials to participate. At the appointed hour, workers, many of whom were women, from different villages, all affiliated with a workers'

[1] Gandhi said this in a 1925 speech to college students in Trivandrum.

group called the Bihar Manrega Watch (BMW) showed up at the venue, a patch of unclaimed land by some fields. Meetings like this usually follow a familiar pattern: first, there's some call-and-response sloganeering. Arms aloft, fists clenched, somebody would, for instance, shout 'Ladenge!' (We will fight!); this would then be followed by a roar, 'Jeetenge!' (We will win!) Next, the workers sing songs of struggles, and sometimes make speeches, all interspersed with more sloganeering.

As the day wore on, it became evident that the bureaucrats who were invited would not show up. Somewhat unexpectedly, however, an uninvited representative of the local government did show up. This was the mukhiya, elected head of the village council, who was also the most powerful man in the village. He was known to be corrupt, a key reason he had not received an invitation to the meeting. On reaching the venue, he barely paused to take in the crowd—this protesting band of loud but peaceful mazdoors—and, with a few henchmen in tow, tore into them. As a participant at the meeting told me later, the mukhiya 'beat up the mazdoors with his bare hands'.

This is a book about mukhiyas, but even more so about mazdoors. In village politics, the mukhiyas have been the insiders among insiders, often born into wealth and belonging to dominant castes, amassing power and influence. They run local government, allocate funds and profoundly shape the lives of the poor. The mazdoors are anonymous outsiders, on the margins of society: Dalits, women, backward castes, daily-wage labourers.

This book is also about a cast of characters who are neither insiders nor outsiders. Since independence, but even more so in the past few decades, there has been a slow chipping away at old feudal relations in villages. The distinctions between insiders and outsiders are neither clear nor static: some insiders are more on the inside than others; other insiders feel more like outsiders; many outsiders aspire to be, and sometimes become, insiders; and, just as in the case of insiders, there are tiers of outsiders.

The mukhiya and the mazdoor represent two ends of a spectrum in considerable flux.

Up until the age of twenty-three, I was a stranger to Bihar. I was brought up in Manipal, a small university town, and went to college in Delhi. Yet, in my first few months in Bihar, many mistook me for a local, because my first name, Sharan, was a not entirely uncommon surname. '*Saran-ji, Bihar main kahaan padta hai ghar aapka?*' (Where in Bihar are you from?) I would be asked, and I would have to explain that I was an outsider. In those initial days, Bihar had seemed bewildering and distant. Moreover, to the mazdoors of Muzaffarpur, whom I had met within a couple of months of living in Bihar, Karnataka was as foreign as Kiribati. Yet, over time, both Bihar and I grew more familiar with each other. One morning in 2017, as I was hurrying along the path to the BMW office in the village of Ratnauli, Somariya Devi, a mazdoor with long, braided grey hair and a mischievous twinkle, asked: '*Saran-ji, bhoj nahin khilaaye?*' (Saran-ji, will you not hold a feast for us?) How was it, she wondered, that I had got married in the past year and had not yet thrown her a celebration dinner?

I may have still been an outsider to Bihar, but in that moment, as I watched her smile and groped for a wisecrack response, it felt a little like home.

Since 2012, when I first lived in Bihar, there have been two broad reasons for my continued engagement with it. First, the research. I began as a research associate on a study that evaluated a computerised wage-payment system for rural wage workers under the NREGA. In the year 2009, the NREGA had been renamed MGNREGA, where M and G stood for Mahatma Gandhi. In the villages of Bihar, it used to be called Narega, but is now increasingly known as Manrega.[2]

This was not my first brush with the NREGA or village governments: I had previously worked on another study in Andhra Pradesh that focused on the role of women leaders in villages and their impact on the implementation of the Act. However, the scope of the Bihar study—it was spread across thousands of villages in twelve districts—guaranteed that my fieldwork was intense and wide-ranging. I gained access to a kaleidoscopic range of actors, mostly insiders, meeting everyone from the casual wage labourer in the village to the rural development department secretary in the magisterial Old Secretariat building in Patna. I met panchayat heads and activists, block development officers (BDOs)—the most powerful bureaucrat in a block, which is roughly fifteen panchayats—and old Left-party leaders, youth entrepreneurs and Patna's landed elite. This exposure expanded my research interests. Over the years, I graduated to working on topics beyond the NREGA, to focus on local politics, caste, reservations and transparency in government. My research is typical of any quantitatively trained economist, relying on datasets ranging from primary surveys to 'big' administrative data.

The second, and more important, reason for my deep engagement with Bihar is the friends I made there. Several co-researchers have turned out to be people I have formed lasting links with, extending well beyond the scope of our professional

[2] In this book, I will use NREGA to describe the Act and the scheme, unless I am quoting someone else.

friendship. However, the most unusual bond I forged was by happenstance, and unconnected to the world of my research—with Sanjay Sahni and the people's movement he founded in Muzaffarpur, of which BMW was a part. We came from entirely different worlds. Sanjay and I grew up in almost diametrically opposite parts of India (south-west vs north-east), spoke different tongues, were brought up to eat, behave and think differently. The economic gulf between us remains vast. Yet, we became fast friends, bound by affection, ideology, and my respect for him and the inspirational mazdoors—mostly women—who have journeyed alongside him.

At a broad level, this book tells a set of stories on village politics in twenty-first-century Bihar through two distinct yet deeply linked narratives: first, through Sanjay Sahni, who, over the course of the past decade, went from being a road-side electrician in Janakpuri, Delhi, to becoming the leader of an important people's movement. The story of Sahni and the people's movement of Muzaffarpur—one I have been closely associated with since 2012—presents a citizen-side perspective of the local state.[3] The movement is dominated by women and members of Backward and Dalit castes. They collectively organise, staging meetings, awareness drives, protests and rallies to move an apathetic state apparatus to deliver what is theirs by right. This is, therefore, a story of outsiders clamouring for respect, attention and benefits.

[3] I use both 'local state' and 'local government' in this book. Usually, the former is used to refer to the state as an organisation, in the abstract. The latter refers to the specific set of individuals who control the state apparatus at any given point in time.

The second narrative shines a light from within on village local government. India's over 6.6 lakh villages belong to roughly 2,50,000 gram panchayats (GPs), the most basic units of local administration. The focus here is on those who run GPs: the village mukhiya—the most powerful person in village politics—and ward members, village council members. The mukhiyas, who represent 2,500–3,000 households, mostly come from the dominant caste in the GP. The ward members, in comparison, come from a variety of castes and represent constituencies as tiny as 200 households. Consequently, they are far less powerful than the mukhiyas. Indeed, some among them, especially from more disadvantaged backgrounds, lie closer to the mazdoors on the insider–outsider spectrum.

The book alternates between these two narratives, of the mazdoors of the people's movement and the leaders who make up village local government, relying on anecdote and research, stories and data. Together, and in its entirety, I hope the words here approximate something of what life is like in Bihar's villages.

My attempt is not to reach for an overarching theory of how society—specifically, village society—functions, but rather to explore several themes related to the political economy of villages in Bihar. Nor is this book a diary or a chronological account of my many years of living and working in Bihar.

In writing it, I tried to follow a style that the economist Albert Hirschman endorsed in his brilliant 1970 essay 'The Search for Paradigms as a Hindrance to Understanding'. Following Hirschman, I eschewed exciting, novel 'insights' for facts, and forwent theory for stories. This was partly because I am not sure I am the type of scholar capable of formulating a theory of anything, let alone the *entire* rural political economy of Bihar. In addition, I believe it would be a travesty to rein Bihar in.

To straitjacket its trajectory—full of chaos and brilliant humanity—into neat, summarisable boxes would be doing disservice to it.

To borrow from, and adapt, Hirschman, the truth of village life and politics in Bihar, it seemed to me, lay in 'the feeling of it'. In the end, this is what I have attempted to convey throughout: a *feeling* for what I saw.

'Since [2010], however, Bihar lost the plot again,' writes the journalist and writer, M. Rajshekhar, in his terrific book *Despite the State*.[4]

My work in Bihar was entirely in the post-2010 era. I arrived in Patna at the tail end of a tremendous—and largely positive—transformative five years in Bihar's history. Nitish Kumar had just begun his second stint in power after a buoyant first term that had, by many accounts, yanked the state out of the apparent darkness of the Jungle Raj of the Lalu Prasad Yadav years. (This binary itself is not entirely accurate, as Jeffrey Witsoe has documented and we will see in Chapter 4.) When I first lived in Patna, great progress was a recent memory and hope still rampant. Bihar was galloping towards the future, a golden era that harkened back to its greatest years. Perhaps, with only slight exaggeration, even the Mauryan Era of the third century BCE.

And yet, within a decade, as Rajshekhar writes, the dreams faded, the plot was lost.

[4] M. Rajshekhar, *Despite the State: Why India Lets Its People Down and How They Cope*, Context/Westland, Chennai, p. 155.

How this came to be is beyond the scope of this book.[5] Echoes of great disappointment, dashed hopes and deep suffering are strewn throughout these pages: these will, upon extrapolation, hint at the various social, political and economic factors responsible for how and why things have changed. However, the various political and social forces at the state and national levels–the centralisation of power, the muzzling of the media, the rise of majoritarian politics, the constant shifting of political alliances, the specious social media propaganda–are either entirely absent or only briefly touched upon here. Of the three major policy questions that Bihar faced over the past decade–the alcohol ban, handling the fallout of demonetisation and GST and dealing with the pandemic–this book only addresses the last.

Look under the broad, sweeping narratives, say, of rising majoritarianism or a collapsing economy, and you will find swirling, vivid sub-narratives that escape easy categorisations. This book dwells on a subset of these arcs, those that are salient to the stories of the insiders and outsiders I focus on. A host of larger-than-life political figures–from Gandhi to Ambedkar, Lalu Yadav and Nitish Kumar–make appearances, often on multiple occasions, in these pages. But their presence is largely in service of the micro-narratives I am focused on. This is not to suggest that the minuscule and the grand are separate objects: the former both affects and is affected by the latter.

---

[5] One of the best social scientists studying modern Bihar is Awanish Kumar. His writings over the past decade in the *Economic and Political Weekly* offer a great starting point to understanding power, caste, development and state-level politics in the Nitish Kumar years. See: Awanish Kumar, 'Where Is Caste in Development?', *Economic and Political Weekly*, Vol. 50, No. 45, 2015, https://www.epw.in/node/146046/pdf, and Awanish Kumar, 'Nitish Kumar's Triumph', *Economic and Political Weekly*, Vol. 45, No. 48, 2010, pp. 7-8.

To state the obvious, Bihar is no monolith. Even if it may seem like the state has lost the plot since 2010, the many Bihars it encompasses have trajectories that are not unidirectional, remain eternally fascinating and merit recording.

This book deals with a range of broad themes that are relevant to village politics, both in Bihar and elsewhere. It does no more than offer a glimpse into some of these themes, dealing with them only insofar as they further the narrative. Several of them are complex and have been the subject of both public debate and much scholarship. For instance, the meat of Chapter 4 is the battle for reservations in favour of Dalits for the post of the village mukhiya. Here, I trace the arguments for and against reservations in Bihar as they played out in the courts and the legislature. While I do speak of Dalits more broadly, the chapter is no more than a drop in the ocean that is the Dalit question. Wherever possible, I have pointed the interested reader to broader writings on these issues. The selection of writings I refer the reader to reflect my own biases, as I am trained mainly in economics. On many topics—caste, clientelism, collective action, panchayati raj institutions—sociology, anthropology and political science offer great insight.

Similarly, the Muzaffarpur movement I document here is not the first of its kind, even in Bihar. The extraordinary work of the Jan Jagaran Shakti Sangathan (JJSS) in east Bihar is but one example of a group of driven individuals collectively mobilising against an apathetic state. Peaceful collective action and protest is a tradition that goes all the way back to Gandhi via the likes of the Mazdoor Kisan Shakti Sanghathan (MKSS), the Narmada Bachao Andolan, the Namantar Andolan and older trade union struggles.

Up until February 2019, as a PhD student, I had pursued two different strands of issues related to local government in Bihar: first, the role of Bihar's recently launched grievance redressal system in furthering transparency in government and resolving 'last-mile' issues in delivery of benefits to citizens. A grievance redressal system is a formal mechanism that allows citizens to complain against the state. Citizens across the world use such systems to flag issues like a malfunctioning streetlight, a broken sidewalk or poor distribution of benefits. Bihar, under Nitish Kumar, had launched a complaints system that, on paper at least, seemed quite powerful.

I had arrived at grievance redressal systems through the researching of social audits. I was, and remain, impressed by the work of the Society for Social Audits, Accountability and Transparency (SSAAT) in Andhra Pradesh. When I first arrived in Bihar, I attended public hearings conducted by activists in Araria and Muzaffarpur. For many working in the area of transparency in government, there is a straight line that connects audits and public hearings to grievance redressal systems.[6]

Alongside studying grievance redressal systems, I had pursued a line of research on elected officials in local government, focusing on mukhiyas and ward members. Given how the power structure within local government greatly favoured mukhiyas, it seemed to me that devolution of more powers—administrative, but also financial—to ward members may serve to balance the power concentrated in the hands of the mukhiyas.

One afternoon in February 2019, as I navigated Patna's Boring Road, a thought struck me: Bihar had a grievance

[6] A forthcoming book on transparency in government, focusing on the work of SSAAT, is Rajesh Veeraraghavan's enlightening *Patching Democracy: Informational Politics and Social Change in India. (Oxford University Press, Modern South Asia Series, 2021)*

redressal system that promised much and solved about a third of the citizens' complaints. This was quite impressive for such systems in India, even more so for a poor state like Bihar. The ward members, who were largely rendered powerless, did have complaints. Could they use the grievance redressal system to lobby on behalf of their constituents? Were they already doing so? These questions soon took over my PhD and much of my waking days. What I learnt over the next few years forms most of chapters 5 and 6. Taken together, these two chapters peer into the local state, telling the story of marginal insiders negotiating their way through a labyrinthine beast.

In the end, though, I return to the marginal outsider, the 'last among equals'. The economist-activist Jean Drèze wrote in his collection of essays, *Sense and Solidarity*, that the local government structures are 'anti-worker' and marked by 'indifference if not deep hostility towards marginalised people in general and rural workers in particular'.[7] I look at how powerful insiders use the system to crush collective action attempts by the outsiders. Activists all around–and academics like Drèze–will be familiar with this arc, featuring fake first information reports (FIRs), invented testimonies, arbitrary red-tapism and seeded discord. These responses, brutal and predictable, hark back to those of the colonial state in the pre-independence era. Many movements wither away, unable to withstand the relentless assault of the state: the Muzaffarpur movement's spirited response makes up the final portions of the book.

---

[7] Jean Drèze, *Sense and Solidarity: Jholawala Economics for Everyone*, Orient Blackswan, New Delhi, 2017, p. 143.

In the essay quoted earlier, Hirschmann also wrote: 'He who looks for large-scale social change must be possessed ... by "the passion for what is possible" rather than rely on what has been certified as probable ...'

In the 1990s, Bihar saw social churn through political action. Under Lalu Yadav, the writ of the old upper-caste elites was challenged by a group of empowered dominant backward castes. In this book, set in the post-Nitish Kumar era, I document four other ways through which entrenched power structures in villages were gradually being dismantled: reservations, decentralisation, higher bureaucratic mandate and collective action.

This book shows that social change at scale can come about through government action. The Seventy-third and Seventy-fourth Amendments to the Indian Constitution, passed by the Parliament in 1992, empowered local government institutions and have had far-reaching consequences. Devolution of power to the lowest tiers of the Indian state is still a work in progress, but even the amendments' worst critics will agree that they have made India's democracy more representative. Bihar's own experiments with political reservations and political decentralisation serve to give voice to those previously disenfranchised.

India has gifted the world another tradition of bringing about social and political change at scale. This is through sustained collective mobilisation of the masses, a distinct feature of the freedom struggle. The Muzaffarpur people's movement is a descendant, like thousands of others since independence, of the national movement.

In the villages of Bihar, those on the margins–women, old, disabled, Dalit, extremely backward castes–find that the *certified probabilities* for their upliftment are small. And yet, incredibly, members belonging to these very groups, dreaming of bringing about lasting social change, form the core of the people's movement of Muzaffarpur. Their 'passion for what is possible' is electric. One has to be there to see it.

If, in these pages, I have managed to convey some of what this *feels* like, I would consider this a successful endeavour.

1

A Movement Is Born

I first met Sanjay Sahni in 2012. Somewhat short and wiry, he sported a pencil moustache. His oiled hair was shabbily parted to one side. He wore, if I recall correctly, mostly off-white shirts and brown pants. You could not tell him apart from any of the young local volunteers of the Jan Jagaran Shakti Sangathan.

It had rained all week in Araria: the trees, rejuvenated, shone anew, their leaves glistening. It was Sanjay's first time there, and mine too. We were there to learn. My interests were vague and academic, being as I was an employed researcher studying government programmes in Bihar. Sanjay's interests were straightforward: he ran a movement of his own and he was there to learn techniques he could adopt to help his saathis, comrades, back home in Muzaffarpur. Sanjay scarcely made an impression on anyone that time. He hung around at the back and barely spoke a word as, over the week, we witnessed fiery plays in street corners and lantern-lit public meetings in villages.

In smaller groups, he spoke a little more. He insisted that, on our way back to Patna, my friend Ani and I stop by his village. Sanjay was persistent, his sunken eyes shining: 'You have to see what we do!' I remember being both impressed by his perseverance and, yet, sceptical of what we would see. Given all that we had witnessed and learnt over the past week, I feared a damp end to a wonderful week. Nonetheless, half-reluctantly, we decided to make a quick stop.

As the train to Muzaffarpur chugged along, seated in the unreserved compartment, and squeezed between men and women and suitcases of all sizes, Sanjay told us his story.

And what a story it was.

In the year 2011, Sanjay Sahni was living what was, in his words, an 'araam zindagi', a contented life.[8] He was an electrician, with a road-side establishment, a khokha, on the streets of Janakpuri in Delhi. He had a steady stream of clients and made Rs 600-700 a day. He was married with two young children.

Every few months, Sanjay would take the Bihar Sampark Kranti from New Delhi to Muzaffarpur, often travelling unreserved, to see his parents in Ratnauli.

Like so many Bihar villages, Ratnauli can be picturesque, nondescript and unsightly all at the same time.

The road to the village is breathtaking: one encounters green paddy fields on either side; trees, tall and handsome, kissing the skies; silver ponds where buffaloes and kids bathe. A lone tea stall, with thick white smoke emanating from its confines, announces that you have arrived. Within the village, plain, unpainted brick houses—dung adorning some walls—all huddled together like bodies around a fire on winter nights. The lanes are mostly kuccha, untarred, punctuated by potholes and the odd open drain.

---

[8] This is a direct quote from Sanjay's talk during the session on 'Reflections on Technology and Transformation' at the 'Re-wiring Women's Rights Debates in the Digital Age' short course organised by IT for Change, Bengaluru, 13 September 2014.

Navigating these lanes in late 2011, Sanjay encountered a few mazdoors talking among themselves. He stopped to eavesdrop. They were clearly agitated, complaining of unpaid wages.

He then heard a word that, by virtue of its foreignness, stuck: *Narega.*

Narega is colloquialism for the National Rural Employment Guarantee Act, a phonetic verbalisation of its acronym.[9] Dubbed the 'largest anti-poverty programme in the world', at its core, the NREGA embodies a deceptively simple yet powerful idea: 'Ask for work and it will be given.'

Why is this important?

Two-thirds of India lives in its villages. The majority of workers in India's villages are involved in agriculture. Agriculture is seasonal: during sowing and harvest, work begins at the crack of dawn and ends as the sun sinks. Between these periods, in the summer months particularly, life slows down: for men who stay behind in their villages, the day begins late and is partitioned by long post-prandial siestas. Others are found engaging in leisurely card games; children while time away in carefree play or, as was the fashion until the government banned the app, find a smartphone and make TikTok videos; women still wake before most and work long, but time is less scarce.

[9] An excellent recent contribution on the politics of the NREGA is Rob Jenkins and James Manor, *Politics and the Right to Work: India's National Rural Employment Guarantee Act*, Oxford University Press, New York, 2017. An early, comprehensive work on the NREGA in Bihar that remains relevant even seven years after publication is P. Dutta, R. Murgai, M. Ravallion and D. Van de Walle, *Right to Work? Assessing India's Employment Guarantee Scheme in Bihar*, World Bank Publications, Washington DC, 2014. For a primer on the early years of the NREGA across India, see the excellent 2011 edited volume by Reetika Khera, *The Battle for Employment Guarantee*, Oxford University Press, New Delhi, 2011.

This gentler pace of life would have been welcome if it came with no riders. The absence of steady employment (or any at all) has implications for how lives are lived. Food is rationed and meals are skipped. Unexpected emergencies, more common than you would imagine, make loans at alarming interest rates a necessity. In Muzaffarpur, the month of May coincides with the annual arrival of the deadly encephalitis virus. As one woman from the village of Agha Nagar told me: 'The babies weep, their heads growing big with fever; and then, if you don't take them to a hospital soon enough, they are gone.'

The need for guaranteed employment–a 'right to work'–was part of policy debates as far back as when the nation was conceived, with the likes of Dr B.R. Ambedkar strongly advocating for it to be enshrined in the Constitution. However, as social scientists R. Jenkins and J. Manor note: 'the genesis of what would become NREGA stemmed from the interrelation between economic realities in Rajasthan and political developments in Delhi'.[10] In Rajasthan in 2001, 'several activist groups ... connected to but extending far beyond the MKSS, began articulating a demand that the state government pass an employment guarantee act.'[11] This sustained pressure, first in Rajasthan, then throughout the country, coincided with the surprise victory of the United Progressive Alliance (UPA) in the general elections in 2004. The UPA had some obvious pro-poor leanings, and had even promised the creation of an employment guarantee programme in their manifesto. On 5 September 2005, in the relatively short span of sixteen months since the alliance formed a government, the NREGA passed into law.

---

[10] Rob Jenkins and James Manor, 'Act of Creation', *Politics and the Right to Work: India's National Rural Employment Guarantee Act*, Oxford University Press, New York, 2017, p.12.

[11] Ibid.

Not everyone was delighted. *The Economist* magazine was dismissive, saying that the Act was 'guaranteed to disappoint'.[12] An Indian commentator called it the 'mother of all sops' and that it could 'bankrupt the government'.[13]

On the other hand, Jean Drèze called it a 'victory for democracy', a 'tool for empowerment' and 'as the potential foundation of a permanent social security system in rural India'.[14]

On paper at least, there were three things the NREGA got right.

First, *anybody* could walk up to their village head and demand work. In other words, the Act was *universal* and gave workers a statutorily enshrined *right* to work. This was, therefore, a justiciable right: if the local administration could not provide work within fifteen days, aggrieved citizens could take the government to court.

Second, the Act was designed to exclude the rich and include the poor. The type of work provided under it would involve hard, 'unskilled' labour. The work is termed 'unskilled' because it requires no formal training. However, as the software engineer-turned-social scientist Rajesh Veeraraghavan found out

---

12 See here: 'Guaranteed to Disappoint', *The Economist*, 29 December 2004, https://www.economist.com/asia/2004/12/29/guaranteed-to-disappoint.

13 Shankkar Aiyar, 'NREGS could be world's biggest social security initiative, but needs transparency', *India Today*, 12 September 2005, https://www.indiatoday.in/magazine/nation/story/20050912-national-rural-employment-guarantee-scheme-787059-2005-09-12.

14 Jean Drèze, 'Democracy and the Right to Work', *Peace Magazine*, 1 January 2006, http://peacemagazine.org/archive/v22n1p20.htm.

after trying to dig bunds on an NREGA worksite, the word may be a misnomer. He writes:[15]

> Digging bunds involves breaking up the ground, removing stones, and carrying and depositing sand. I wanted to prove that I could do it, without realizing that by doing so I would become a laughing stock in the group and later in the village... I soon realized that I did not have the skill required to do what the government classifies as 'unskilled' labor. The woman [an NREGA labourer who had offered to teach him] was patient and said she would show me how to use the tools to work properly. I poked around and narrowly escaped chopping off my leg several times, worrying all the time about flying pieces of stone from nearby digging hitting my eyes. I worked dutifully for a bit, but the sun was very hot, and I already felt that it had been a long session of hard manual labour. Thus, those unaccustomed to doing such work wouldn't apply for it in the first place. Beneficiaries, therefore, would comprise largely landless poor.

Third, the Act marked a major landmark in furthering transparency in government. From the outset, the NREGA website–www.nrega.nic.in–logged every single day of work done by any individual in any part of the country. This was accessible to all. To this day, sitting in Delhi or Chennai or Davangere, one can see *who* did *how much* work on *what* NREGA worksite in, say, Sutihara or Phulera.

None of these ideas travelled seamlessly from paper to reality.

For one, even to this day, work on demand is extremely unlikely. In most cases, the local government *bestows* work on the needy.

---

[15] R. Veeraraghavan, 'Open Governance and Surveillance: A Study of The National Rural Employment Program in Andhra Pradesh, India', UC Berkeley, p. 84, https://escholarship.org/uc/item/3805n440.

Also, while the rich had no interest in doing the work, it did not stop them from them having their names put on the rolls and siphoning off money (a trend that was particularly rampant in the early years).

And lastly, while the NREGA website is indeed a vast treasure trove of information, it is not always accurate. Indeed, as anthropologist Nayanika Mathur argues in her sobering, although not entirely bleak, anthropological examination of the Indian state in Uttarakhand, the NREGA's 'asli zindagi', or real life, differed considerably from its 'sarkari zindagi', or government life.

It was a chance discovery of the vast gap between these two zindagis of the NREGA that overturned Sanjay Sahni's araam zindagi, propelling him from electrician of Janakpuri to mazdoor-activist of Ratnauli.

Delhi's Janakpuri was showcased in loving montages in the 2010 Bollywood sleeper hit, *Band Baaja Baaraat*. In it, we catch glimpses of this quintessential West Delhi locality: bustling, crowded and dusty, with walls often serving as partitions between eras: an old-school family-run saree shop will sit adjacent to a showroom selling the swankiest of cars; an electrician plying his wares on the street will boast an air-conditioned cybercafe for a neighbour.

Around the time that movie released, Sanjay Sahni, electrician of Janakpuri, could not help but notice people streaming into the cybercafe neighbouring his khokha. He would often sneak a glance inside as he passed the establishment. It seemed to be perpetually teeming with young women and men—many his own age—lost in the wonders of their virtual worlds.

One evening, when work was slow, Sanjay gathered the courage to enter that cybercafe. He positioned himself near the entrance, next to where the owner, a Sikh gentleman, sat. The owner, who knew him by sight, asked Sanjay what he was doing there. In Delhi, the city of outsiders, some were more on the fringe than others. Sanjay Sahni, of oiled hair, rough hands and stilted tongue, simply did not look like he belonged to the world of cyber-surfing.

Sanjay nonchalantly responded that he was doing nothing. Just looking. The owner was not impressed, but let him linger.

The observant young electrician watched intently: those surfing would typically tap the gol chakri, round wheel, at the bottom of the screen. This would cause a box to pop up. They would then type something in the box; and off they went, reading text, watching videos, playing games.

The box, Sanjay realised, held the key.

In 1998, Larry Page and Sergey Brin had invented a search engine that transformed how information would be classified in the virtual and real worlds. Thirteen years later—by when 'Google' had been verbified—Sanjay Sahni gaped in awe at the search-bar and the gol chakri, the Google Chrome icon, that seemed to serve as a portal to a vast, new world.

Emboldened by a deep desire to know, Sanjay slunk into a seat that had just seen a customer leave. The owner noticed. He tried to shoo him off. Sanjay, once more, said he was doing nothing, just checking. Mouse in hand, Sanjay clicked frantically, arbitrarily. At first, there was nothing. Then, it happened: the gol chakri transformed into a box.

Sanjay could spell his name in English. He could even read and write, if somewhat slowly. He typed, letter by letter, these words: *Bihar narega.*

I have asked Sanjay what made him type those words. He said he wanted to type something important or official-sounding, worthy of a computer. Elsewhere, he has said that he was curious about the foreign word 'narega' that seemed to be the cause of much agitation. I imagine it also had the flavour of something familiar, rhyming closely with a string of the most common Hindi verbs (karega, darega), and yet, like a thought that had momentarily escaped one's mind, felt just out of grasp.

A few more clicks and Sanjay found himself on the NREGA website. It was mainly in English, which slowed down his progress. The owner's patience was running thin. Eventually, he asked Sanjay to leave. Sanjay requested two minutes more, scanning the entire web page for something to hold on to.

And then he spotted it. In a corner, sandwiched between 'Munger' and 'Nalanda', was a familiar name: Muzaffarpur. His heart racing, he clicked on it. He then saw another unfamiliar set of names in English, but soon he found his block (Kurhani) and then, with another click, he navigated to his panchayat (Ratnauli). One final click more and, suddenly, he saw names, not of places, but of people. The first name he saw–etched clearly in his mind almost a decade later–was 'Mahender Paswan'. As he went down the list, he saw more names, all familiar: 'It was like I was sitting in Delhi, but also in my village.'

It is worth, if only briefly, pausing to consider how momentous and confusing all of this must have felt. The Indian state draws its awesome power from meticulous record-keeping that it stows away in a tower of obfuscations. In his ten-minute jaunt through the world wide web, Sanjay had stumbled upon the tower, found a virtual entrance and had navigated to precisely the location where vaults stored information about his village.

Sanjay was in a frenzy. He asked the owner to print every web page related to his village. The owner asked him if he had gone mad. There were hundreds of pages of names. It would cost Rs 450, three-quarters of Sanjay's daily earnings. Sanjay was unfazed. The owner's incredulity gave way to joy.

This decision to print everything was driven by a mix of uncertainty and astuteness. There were two sources of uncertainty: first, he was not sure the information would be there the next time he got to the website; second, he was not even sure he could navigate to the website in the first place. He needed to have everything in print.

Sanjay was also perceptive enough to know that the records were not all benign. The documents—entirely in Hindi—did not merely contain names, but descriptions of projects undertaken and wages paid under NREGA. These were, therefore, wage rolls; or, in the language of NREGA, *muster rolls*. Sanjay spent much of the night going over the records: he was onto something and would get to the bottom of it.

The next morning, when the owner arrived at his cybercafe, he found Sanjay waiting. There was a marked difference in how Sanjay was treated now, with the owner calling him 'beta', son, and ushering him inside with an invitation to sit: *Baith, baith, baith, baith.*

To his relief, Sanjay found that he was able to retrace his steps from the previous day. He clicked around on the NREGA website and found a mobile number on a contact page. He called the number and the man at the other end—a certain Rajeev Sharma—said that he was based in Rajasthan and could not help someone in Bihar. Instead, he offered another phone number, that of the activist and NREGA-pioneer Nikhil Dey.

Sanjay called the number. Dey answered and apologetically told him that he was travelling that week, and asked Sanjay to call him back. Over the next four weeks, Sanjay would call Dey ever so often, only to be told that the latter was busy. Fed up, he reverted to calling Rajeev Sharma, the man from Rajasthan, who asked him to call yet another number. This turned out to be of a certain Mohammed Afzal from Maharashtra, who politely told Sanjay that he was posted in Maharashtra and gave him the number of someone else who may help. Sanjay called the number and realised he was calling, once more, Nikhil Dey, his old evasive friend. Exhausted, Sanjay gave up. He stopped calling.

Instead, he decided to go to his village and investigate the matter on his own.

On the train back home, the questions kept playing in his mind: What were these documents? Why were there so many names? Why was there so much money—often in the thousands—against all these names? What did it mean when the labourers said they did not get paid? Where was the money?

On reaching his village, Sanjay lost no time in making enquiries. Documents in hand, he went to the tola, or hamlet, closest to his home and tracked down the names from the wage rolls, asking if they had been paid the amount mentioned in the documents. No sooner did he begin than Sanjay noticed the most powerful man in the village, the village mukhiya, trailing him.

The mukhiya, whom I had met once, was a large man, his size accentuated by the relatively shorter average heights of rural Bihar folk. He sported a greying moustache and was almost completely bald, which made him resemble, in one chronicler's words, 'the actor Amrish Puri at his most villainous'.[16]

Sanjay, speaking about this first encounter with the mukhiya two years later, described it thus:

> The mukhiya asked me, kindly at first: 'Where have you got these papers from?'

---

16 S. Denyer, *Rogue Elephant: Harnessing the Power of India's Unruly Democracy*, Bloomsbury Press, New York, 2014, p. 142.

> 'Where? I got them from Delhi.'
>
> 'You are making a mistake. You do not know what you are getting into. You keep these papers at home. You are making a good salary in Delhi, you should go back there. Don't get involved in these things.'
>
> I said I was not getting into anything.
>
> A few minutes of back and forth later, the mukhiya lost his temper and insulted me in the worst possible manner. The documents were all muster rolls—payments for labourers, fakes he had created. Seeing these with me made him angry. He followed me all the way home and threatened me. He even found my parents, scolded them and said: 'Your son will be destroyed. Send him back to Delhi.'

Sanjay's parents were worried. The mukhiya was also a Sahni, though the families were not very close: a vast economic gulf separated them. Sahnis, traditionally fishermen (or practising fishing-related occupations like net-weaving), are officially classified as Extremely Backward Classes (EBCs) in Bihar. Most Sahnis are poor, occupying the bottom few rungs of the wealth ladder. However, owing to their large numbers in certain pockets in North Bihar, some among them, like the mukhiya of Ratnauli, had become local strongmen and muscled their way through to power.[17] This was not the case with Chandra Shekhar Sahni, Sanjay's father. He had spent most of his life as a migrant labourer in cities like Calcutta and Ranchi. In the

[17] Sahnis come from the Nishad community, a collection of sub-castes that are often found along villages that border the rivers flowing through Central and North Bihar. The prominent Nishad sub-castes are Mallah, Godhi, Sahni, Kevat and Noniya. Roughly 30 per cent of the households of Ratnauli are Sahnis. The Sahnis of Ratnauli are, on average, economically as badly off as the Dalits. However, a handful of wealthy Sahni households dominate political life.

light of such obvious disparities, the senior Sahni persuaded his son to leave the village and return to the city.

Back in Delhi, Sanjay returned to his old life. One day, on a whim, he tried Nikhil Dey's number again. To his surprise, Dey said he was in Delhi and could meet. Sanjay remembers hastily packing his tools, closing his khoka and rushing to Hauz Khas, his precious printouts in hand. He was relieved when Dey, after listening to Sanjay and scrutinising the documents, declared that this was indeed evidence of corruption. Later, acknowledging Sanjay's resoluteness, Dey wrote that that the young man 'doggedly pursued this trail until he tracked us down, and two months later he made sure that we met him and heard his story'.[18]

Dey then put Sanjay in touch with A. Santhosh Mathew–a bureaucrat known for his dynamism and heart–who was then the principal secretary to the Rural Development Department in Bihar. Mathew asked Sanjay to meet him the next time he made his way back to Bihar.

Sanjay caught the first train out of Delhi and showed up at Mathew's doorstep.

I asked Mathew if he remembered that first meeting.

'What do you mean by "remember the meeting"?' he asked in a manner that implied the answer was obvious. Sanjay was among those people 'who leave a mark on your psyche', Mathew explained. '[Sanjay's] was a remarkable story ... He was just *struck* by the exploitation but also the falsification of records.'

[18] Nikihil Dey, 'The Answers Are Blowing in the Wind', Jan Jagaran Shakti Sangathan, 24 January 2014, https://jjssbihar.wordpress.com/2014/01/24/the-answers-are-blowing-in-the-wind/.

As a civil servant, Mathew had been involved in designing the NREGA, and had long recognised its potential. In Sanjay, he saw someone who shared that sentiment: 'Here was this man who actually related to that vision and that promise. In him, I saw India's future ... and an important ally to understand the reality on the ground for a scheme I was responsible for the implementation of. What can be greater than that?'

Mathew proposed to send an audit team to Ratnauli. Sanjay was elated, even though he did not fully appreciate what that would entail. In the meanwhile, Mathew said, he would have prominent walls in the village painted with information from muster rolls. When Sanjay reached his village later that evening, he was amazed to see painters diligently painting walls with names and amounts. Mathew had kept his word. Mahender Paswan and the other NREGA labourers of the village had travelled once more–from the web pages discovered in a cybercafe in Delhi to the walls of their own Ratnauli in Muzaffarpur.

On reaching home, Sanjay found the mukhiya waiting at his doorstep. I will, once more, let Sanjay relate the conversation that followed:

> The mukhiya said: 'You are back again!'
>
> I said, 'What can I do? Am I doing anything to you? I have come back to my village–can't I return home?'
>
> 'You are responsible for all this–all the writing on the wall–I know you are making it happen.'
>
> 'Me? Why will I make them write it?

The argument did not last long, but both parties had realised that something new, different, even *dangerous*, was afoot.

The writing was, quite literally, on the wall.

In January 2012, in accordance with Mathew's orders, officials from Patna and Muzaffarpur descended on Ratnauli. It was a cold winter day, smoky and overcast. Sanjay had assembled hundreds of aggrieved villagers. The mukhiya and his henchmen were there too. In the days leading up to the audit, they 'had warned everyone of trouble if they participated and testified', as journalist Simon Denyer reports in his book.[19]

The audit 'began in a tense atmosphere', he says. Government officials read out names, one by one, from the official muster rolls: *so-and-so was paid X thousand rupees.* Seasoned activists such as Dey had told Sanjay that even if one person spoke out, the chances were that 'the floodgates would open, and even the poorest would tell their own stories'.

Soon enough, a name was read out and an activist-lawyer from Ratnauli who was in attendance 'piped up, saying that the man had left the village years ago to live with his in-laws'.

This caused the floodgates to open, but not how Sanjay had expected.

The headman's thugs had had enough. They pounced on the instigator and punched and kicked him. In the chaos that ensued—all in plain view of the auditors—Sanjay was among those who suffered a blow. The government 'suspended the social audit, asked everyone who had gathered to disperse, and ordered the block office to file an FIR report against those who had disrupted it'.[20]

Even a full twelve months later, no such FIR was filed. The state spoke in two voices: what Patna willed, Ratnauli did not.

---

[19] Simon Denyer, *Rogue Elephant: Harnessing the Power of India's Unruly Democracy*, Bloomsbury Press, New York, 2014, p. 142.

[20] Nikhil Dey, 'The Answers Are Blowing in the Wind', JJSS, 24 January 2014, https://jjssbihar.wordpress.com/2014/01/24/the-answers-are-blowing-in-the-wind/.

Seen purely as an exercise in achieving its stated goal of exposing corruption, the audit had failed. However, it had succeeded in an entirely different manner: Sanjay Sahni of Delhi was now known as the man who brought Patna to his village. The mighty state had deigned to descend on Ratnauli and organise an audit, a hitherto impossible achievement. The mukhiya and his henchmen may have thwarted the audit, but they did not escape with their reputations intact: their corrupt acts were now a matter of public discussion. The gamut of local government officials—the mukhiya, the panchayat secretary, the panchayat rozgar sevak (PRS), the BDO—knew that Patna's eyes were on them. Most important of all, the women and men of Ratnauli had found their voices.

Sanjay was in a quandary: on the one hand was his life in Delhi, predictable and risk-free; on the other was the prospect of being an activist in Ratnauli, a life both rewarding and unstable.

A return to the village would also necessitate more confrontations with the mukhiya and his henchmen. After the audit, Sanjay's relationship with the mukhiya had soured entirely: a tiny spark might cause the tinderbox to explode. Even if he managed to negotiate those waters, a further—arguably more urgent—problem awaited him: how would an electrician earn in a village with barely any electricity?

Over the next year and more, Sanjay would struggle to resolve these issues: he would shuttle between Delhi and Muzaffarpur, making barely enough to keep his family afloat and boring a hole through his savings; an uneasy peace would reign between periodic flare-ups with the mukhiya. His family was not greatly enthused by this new state of affairs. Nikhil Dey writes about a time when Sanjay's wife, Sarita, called Dey and 'quite bluntly' asked him if working for others must come at the cost of ruining the lives of one's own.

I remember having a long conversation with Sanjay's father around this time. The older Sahni is lean, with long sturdy limbs and greying hair. I asked him if he was proud of his eldest son. His response was a series of counter-questions: Of what use is this pride? What about his family? How will they eat? What about his younger brothers? Who will teach them the trade now? Worse still, will they also neglect their families and fight for others?

I was taken aback by the clarity of his thoughts, the flatness of his voice, his calm. As I took leave in the falling dusk, the only signs of concern I could spot were the worry lines that creased his forehead.

By the time I visited Ratnauli, over a year had passed since Sanjay first typed 'Bihar Narega' on Google.

He had organised a sabha. This was, by his count, the 112th such gathering since his triumphant return to Muzaffarpur. The venue, in the village of Mahant Maniyari, was the portico of an abandoned mansion of sorts, surrounded by green-yellow fields. When we got there, a crowd had already gathered: everywhere there were women, clad in bright saris that acquired a fluorescent halo in the grey light. They were in the front, welcoming us, huddling by the mansion's old pillars, on ledges and stairs. A small group of men also raised their hands in salutation as they saw Sanjay approach.

The sabha was to begin at 11 a.m. Fifteen minutes past the hour, I asked Sanjay if we should start. He laughed and said: '*Abhi aur log aa hi rahen hain*' (People are still coming), and nonchalantly pointed eastwards. I turned to look and was taken aback: there, beyond the fields, in a trail that extended as far as the eye could see, were women and men, walking towards the venue.

When another fifteen minutes had passed and the sabha had finally begun (with people still trickling in), the mazdoors sat in rapt attention, listening to Sanjay. It soon dawned on me that this was no normal audience; this was not NREGA 101 for beginners, it was far more advanced. Participants were aware of their rights under the Act. Sanjay was not preaching but discussing the intricacies of the NREGA. Over the course of the next couple of hours, speeches were made and labourers sang songs of toil they had composed, and we sang songs on rights and injustice that a friend and I had learnt that past week in Araria.

It was clear that the gathering had only one star. Sanjay seemed to have a magnetic influence over his audience. He chided them for being stupid, swelled with pride when they sang. He was their teacher and guide, hero and, as we discovered much to our shock from one of their songs, had been put on the same pedestal as Ram and Sita.

In the past year, the village had transformed considerably: over 700 mazdoors had worked on eight separate NREGA worksites. Most were first-time workers. Payments were still due for some, and local government officials continued to invent innovative hurdles. However, it was also true that the sleeping state had woken. All it took was one computer, one semi-literate man and several hundred, mostly women workers.

Sanjay was no longer a nobody, a city worker with tenuous roots to his village and his people. He was famous in these parts now. The chowk where he held his sabhas had people thronging from afar to catch a glimpse of him. Fittingly, it has been rechristened *NaREGA Chowk*.

In February 2015, at the start of the budget session, Prime Minister Narendra Modi spoke disparagingly of the NREGA in Parliament. The popular English-language magazine, *Outlook*, described the event thus:[21]

> The Prime Minister spoke on whether or not his government would continue the MGNREGA–Congress party's flagship programme guaranteeing 100 days of manual work every year to at least one member of every village household.
>
> With a smirk on his face, Modi asked: 'Do you think I will disband the scheme? My political wisdom does not allow me to do it. This is a living monument of your failure to tackle poverty in 60 years.'
>
> He continued: 'You had to send people to dig ditches and pay them. With song and dance and drum beat, I will continue with the scheme.'

Even allowing for a certain degree of hyperbole, this was a fairly strong position to take. However, it was not far from what many, especially those in the cities, felt. By the time 2014 came around, public commentators characterised the NREGA as 'populist, politically motivated and ... beset with corruption and leakages ... [and] responsible for runaway fiscal deficits, inflation and slowdown of growth'.[22]

The academic evidence on the NREGA is more equivocal. Indeed, it is, if anything, optimistic of the Act's ability to

---

[21] Mirza Arif Beg, 'Once Called "Living Monument of UPA's Failures" By PM Modi, Will MGNREGA Help During Covid-19?', *Outlook*, 18 May 2020, https://www.outlookindia.com/website/story/news-analysis-once-called-living-monument-of-upas-failures-by-pm-modi-will-mgnrega-help-during-covid-19/353019.

[22] Dilip Mookherjee, 'MNREGA: Populist leaky bucket or successful anti-poverty programme?', *Ideas for India*, https://www.ideasforindia.in/topics/poverty-inequality/mnrega-populist-leaky-bucket-or-successful-anti-poverty-programme.html.

positively impact the lives of the poor. Summarising nearly a decade's worth of research in the economics of the NREGA, Dilip Mookherjee, professor at Boston University, argued that, while the Act 'was far from perfect in terms of implementation, it was much more effective than other existing schemes in benefiting the poor'. He goes on to say:

> [W]hat seems most striking is the effect of MNREGA in providing a safety net and reducing poverty for the most vulnerable sections of the rural population. Providing employment to rural unskilled labour is without doubt the single most direct and effective way of reducing poverty amongst the most vulnerable sections of the population. Undoubtedly the price tag is large, around 0.4% of GDP. But on the other hand the scheme provides employment to one third of the rural population who are the poorest. With regard to targeting success, it beats hollow the other big-ticket subsidy items in government budgets–food, fertiliser and petroleum subsidies, each of which account for 0.8% of GDP, and benefit mainly the middle class rather than the poor.

Indeed, Mookherjee notes that study after academic study has shown that the NREGA has large impacts on outcomes as diverse as child labour (which fell) and grades in school (large improvements).

A large randomised controlled trial (RCT) in erstwhile united Andhra Pradesh showed arguably the most important result of them all: NREGA improved rural productivity, boosting per-day earnings for *all* rural poor. In other words, the gains were not restricted to only those who worked on it.[23]

---

[23] Karthik Muralidharan, Paul Niehaus, Sandip Sukhtankar, 'General Equilibrium Effects of (Improving) Public Employment Programs: Experimental Evidence from India', 2020, https://econweb.ucsd.edu/~kamurali/Research.html.

In a piece summarising their findings, the authors of the study note: 'We began our own work on the MNREGS[[24]] from a posture of scepticism, documenting corruption and seeking to mitigate it ... but our results from a highly credible, randomised evaluation suggest that MNREGS may be a surprisingly effective tool, both for improving the welfare of the landless rural poor and also increasing overall rural productivity.'[25]

The work of economists and other researchers, thus, for a while ran parallel to popular notions about the scheme. What fuelled this popular narrative of the NREGA, though? Two reasons come to mind: first, the NREGA harmed private land-owner interests across rural India; this class now had to pay higher wages for casual labour. Second, an influential strand of the commentariat in India is deeply influenced by mainstream economics and is suspicious of government, government spending and its ability to intervene meaningfully in the lives of the poor.

I briefly glimpsed the two come together in an encounter with the de facto head (his wife was the de jure head) of a village in Andhra Pradesh. The mukhiya's family, by her husband's own admission, owned hundreds of acres of land around the village. He told me, switching effortlessly from chaste Telugu to fluent English and back, that 'as a fellow economist' (we had both at the time, as we discovered much to his delight, MAs in Economics), it ought to be obvious to us that the NREGA would result in 'rampant inflation and destroy agriculture in

---

[24] The Mahatma Gandhi National Rural Employment Guarantee Scheme, also MGNREGS or NREGS.

[25] Karthik Muralidharan, Paul Niehaus, Sandip Sukhtankar, 'Strengthen MNREGS to support the rural economy', *Ideas for India*, https://www.ideasforindia.in/topics/governance/strengthen-mnregs-to-support-the-rural-economy.html.

India'. He then added, putting his landlord hat on, 'I am, you see, unable to pay for my labour anymore.'

Empirical evidence from ground-level research, which showed how well NREGA actually worked in practice, seemed to have had little impact on popular opinion. However, two dramatic shocks to the Indian economy seem to have changed this discourse somewhat. In the wake of the severe economic contraction caused by demonetisation, the NREGA emerged as a key safety net. Indeed, barely two years after Modi's budget speech, the Finance Ministry's Economic Survey noted that: 'MGNREGS and its implementation by the Government have met the programme's stated role of being a social safety net during times of need.' The irony was not lost on the discerning reader. Not only did the NREGA emerge as the bedrock of the poor, the document lay the credit at the feet of a government the head of which had, not very long ago, characterised the whole Act as a failure.

Nearly four years later, as India suffered a second, more devastating setback and the coronavirus pandemic wrecked livelihoods across the country (and, indeed, the world), a large component of the Union government's relief package was dedicated to the NREGA.

In the warm and winning Amazon Prime series, *Panchayat*, the mukhiya and his council of ward representatives–numbering twelve in total–discuss the matter of installing solar lights in the fictional Uttar Pradesh village of Phulera. The panchayat secretary, a youth from Delhi who is a stand-in for the audience, naively asks everyone to offer suggestions about 'important locations' for the thirteen lights. To his amazement, the mukhiya declares that the only decision to be made is regarding the thirteenth light: '*Baaki ka sab ho gaya hai!*' (The decision on the rest has been made!) It is obvious, the mukhiya explains, that the twelve lights will be placed next to the homes of each of the twelve members of the village council. In the show, this whole scene plays out like farce, and, in the spirit of the material, is casually brushed aside as the conversation moves on to meatier aspects, such as a haunted tree in the village.

Truth is stranger, and deadlier, than fiction: in March 2013, a man was murdered in broad daylight for questioning irregularities in solar light installations in his village. On a pleasant spring evening, five men surrounded the man on an empty village road. They fired two shots, aiming for his belly. The police arrived at the scene and found the victim bleeding profusely. Instead of acting hastily, they took him to a distant hospital in a private vehicle. His brother later said: 'He would have survived had the police taken him to a nearby nursing home. They wanted to kill him.'[26]

The man's name was Ram Kumar Thakur, an upper-caste lawyer and RTI activist from the village of Ratnauli. Through RTIs, he had unearthed a scam in the allocation of solar lights and was also the main witness in an NREGA vigilance case. The police registered an FIR against six persons—the mukhiya of the village and his three sons and two nephews.

Thakur was the brave lawyer-activist who had spoken up at the audit that Sanjay helped convene.

The mukhiya against whom an FIR was registered in connection with his murder was Raj Kumar Sahni. This was the very same man who had, not long ago, threatened to *destroy* Sanjay Sahni.

---

[26] Alok Gupta, 'Blood, Sweat and Tears', *Down To Earth*, 15 May 2013, https://www.downtoearth.org.in/coverage/blood-sweat-and-tears-40911.

2

The Mukhiya Question

District of Bhojpur, 2013, field notes:

We arrange to meet the mukhiya on the highway. It's not quite in the middle of nowhere. In the dim moonlight, we see that the highway is both unexpectedly empty and smooth: someone above must be happy. A car pulls over; it is one of those big cars with three rows of seating. A Maruti Ertiga, Abhishek announces. Abhishek–tall, big-eyed, baby-cheeked–and I are co-workers on a research project. P., our other companion, is my superior.

Four men filter out of the car. One asks us who we are. We say we are researchers and we want to meet the mukhiya. A round of questions follow.

Another man then materialises. He is small and somewhat muscular, in his late twenties and shifty. I am reminded of Aamir Khan in *Ghulam*, only this chap is less conventionally attractive and sports a moustache. 'What do you want?' he asks. We tell him we want to meet the mukhiya, that we had been to his village earlier in the day and had met his brother from whom we obtained a phone number. The mukhiya, we explain to this Bhojpuri Aamir Khan, had spoken to us earlier in the day and we had agreed to meet here, on the highway, adjacent to this school. We had even spoken to him minutes ago on the phone.

The man shoots another quick couple of questions at us before announcing: *I am the mukhiya.*

He invites us inside the car. The invitation echoes from around us; his men seem to like repeating what he says. Abhishek throws me a look of worry. P. who, despite being European, is usually finely attuned to the way of the world in Bihar, says he would rather make conversation outside, on an empty bench. The mukhiya insists. The echoes reinforce it. This is no longer a request.

P. goes in first. Abhishek is next. He gingerly takes his place. I follow. The mukhiya sits in front. His driver is at the wheel and he looks drugged or drunk, I cannot tell. The insides of the car are reasonably well lit, thanks largely to a TV that is playing a documentary of some sort. It is playing at an ear-shattering volume, so the mukhiya asks for it to be paused. As it pauses, we recognise the frozen face on the screen: it is the mukhiya himself.

'Some news channel took a video of me,' he informs us casually.

The three of us do not catch each other's eyes—it is not too dark, but we are sitting beside each other, not across. The car smells of smoke, the mukhiya lights his cigarette.

'So, tell me. What do you want to ask?'

P.'s Hindi is excellent though his accent sometimes comes in the way of comprehension. But there is little difficulty in understanding his first question, worded simply and crisply: 'We had been to your village this morning,' he says. 'And we have come across cases where people who have worked for five days have been shown in the official data as having worked for ten days. And some of the people in the official data don't seem to exist at all.'

This is a pertinent question. But, in the context of things, it feels somewhat cavalier.

If this information was a revelation to the mukhiya, he does not show it.

'Why don't you come back with me?' he counter-questions. 'Let's meet these people again and you can check if there is any mistake?'

P. tells him that that is impossible, we have more work to do the next morning, more villages to visit, more surveys to complete.

The mukhiya then lists his problems with providing work under the NREGA. First, the local bureaucrat handling the NREGA in the village is new, the post office in charge of payments is extremely inefficient. Many times, he himself makes payments to the labourers in advance and gets them to sign on an empty sheet of paper. When the money eventually arrives, he furnishes the sheet at the post office and collects the money.

None of this answers P.'s original question: why is there over-reporting of days in the official data?

But P., undeterred and clearly on a roll here, tells him about a large, isolated hamlet we visited where things were particularly bad. 'Most people have worked barely ten days on the NREGA this year,' he says.

I hear Abhishek let out a sigh.

The mukhiya takes a drag and pauses. He then launches into a tirade against the villagers from the hamlet. They are troublemakers, he spits out. Most of them belong to the 'Ma-Ley' party.

I do not know it then, but Ma-Ley is short for Communist Party of India (Marxist-Leninist) Liberation.

That hamlet has witnessed nine murders, he declares. And mostly, it involves people fighting amongst themselves. '*Lekin*,' he continues, '*hum bhi gaye the, goli-woli chalaaye*.' (I had gone too—fired a few rounds.)

Now, Abhishek finds my hand and gives it a tight squeeze. I cannot remember the last time a grown man had reached for my hand in terror.

The mukhiya explains: 'We need to keep these people under control. They keep raising complaints. A few bullets can only do good.'

Maybe we look shocked, or maybe he thinks we ought to be shocked. So, he explains: 'I am not an honest man. And I won my elections while I was in jail in Jharkhand. If I lived by the book, nothing would happen in the village. It's impossible to pay people on time and it's impossible to control these Ma-Ley people. I fired a few bullets and said that there would no longer be any NREGA work in their hamlet. That seemed to shut them up.'

P. probes a little more, and the mukhiya repeats his request that we spend the night in his village. We politely decline, Abhishek more vehemently than P. or I.

The mukhiya asks: 'So, when do I get to see the report?'

'What report?'

'The report documenting your findings from our village. Isn't the purpose of your research to help us govern better?'

P. explains it would take a while—this is our first exploratory week in a year-long study.

The mukhiya persists: 'Well, who do I get in touch with a year from now?'

'Just call us. You have our number, after all. We spoke on the phone.'

He dishes out his phone, finds the number and asks: 'What name should I save the number under?'

It was Abhishek who had called him earlier in the day. 'Anand,' he replies as coolly as he can. 'Anand is my name.'

Have mukhiyas always been this powerful?

An early authority on local self-government, the political scientist M. Venkatarangaiya,[27] writing in the year 1960,[28] described the history of village self-government as comprising two distinct 'pasts': first, an earlier past that covered the ancient and medieval periods and extended up to 1800; second, a more recent past that ran from about 1800 to 1947. The former past, he argued, enjoyed a more robust form of local self-government, necessitated by isolation. Villages lay beyond the reach of the pre-modern state, and rulers—both Hindu and Muslim—were content to let them be, demanding of them only annual taxes. Thus, the writ of the mukhiyas ran large.

The twin factors of the advent of the British and advances in transport and communication punctured this entrenched status quo. By the 1850s, villages were better connected, and central authorities deployed their own officials in villages—the postman being one such—and gradually eroded the powers of the local state. This profoundly changed the way lives were lived. By 1920, Venkatarangaiya notes, 'the village community was practically broken up and conditions became unfavourable for the successful working of panchayats'. Moreover, mukhiyas had 'ceased to be the natural leaders and representatives of the

---

[27] Mamidipudi Venkatarangaiya, who studied local governments extensively, is my great-grandfather.

[28] M. Venkatarangaiya, 'Local self-government in India', *Quarterly Journal of Local Self-Government Institute*, Bombay, Vol. 31, 1960.

village community and ha[d] become the salaried employees of the central and provincial governments'.[29]

Through the early half of the twentieth century, the man who foremost championed a return to that former past was Mahatma Gandhi. Recognising that 'India lives in its seven and a half lakhs of villages', Gandhi's vision of Swaraj ran bottom-up. He envisaged India as a loose conglomeration of these seven and a half lakh villages, each village a 'republic' in itself. Each village-republic, he said in an interview in 1946, would be 'joined together in ever-widening, *never-ascending*, circles'.[30] (emphasis mine) Thus, Gandhi envisaged India as an open string of beads: a horizontal federation of largely independent villages, with no real centre

This conceptualisation was typically Gandhian, a vision at once radical and conservative. In its rejection of hierarchies and its consequent empowerment of decentralised units, it was anti-statist and progressive. Yet, by romanticising the village as a sanctuary, a bulwark against 'the corrupting effects of modern civilisation', it failed to engage with the ills inherent in village society. Articulating these concerns when the Bombay Legislative Council debated empowerment of panchayats, Dr B.R. Ambedkar famously said:

> A population which is hidebound by caste; a population which is infected by ancient prejudices; a population which flouts equality of status and is dominated by notions of gradations in life; a population which thinks that some are high and some are low—can it be expected to have the right notions even to discharge bare justice? Sir, I deny that

---

[29] M. Venkatarangaiya, 'The Village in the Structure of Local Government', *The Indian Journal of Political Science*, Vol. 4, No. 4, pp. 330–353, 1943.

[30] This quote is from *Harijan* (1946), as retrieved from: https://www.mkgandhi.org/indiadreams/chap25.htm.

> proposition, and I submit that it is not proper to expect us to submit our life, and our liberty, and our property to the hands of these panchas.

When independence came, Ambedkar's disdain for village society and Nehru's faith in a strong central state joined forces to edge out Gandhi's ideals.[31] The latter's vision was relegated to the directive principles, the Indian Constitution's version of a consolation prize.[32]

However, Gandhi's views found support elsewhere: as early as 1947, Bihar set up a Ministry for Local Self Government. The Bihar Panchayat Raj was promulgated in 1948 and made provisions for the posts of mukhiya, sarpanch and dalpati to introduce 'self-rule in villages'.

These moves did not, however, stand much of a chance against the centralising nature of the state, a consequence of the early Nehru years. Between 1947 and 1993, the panchayati raj system–in Bihar and elsewhere–hobbled along. In 1978, the Ashok Mehta Committee on panchayati raj institutions described a sorry state of affairs:

> The disassociation of the growing and complex programme of development with Panchayati Raj Institutions which were considered inadequate, the inability of the bureaucracy to be attuned to execute the programme through elected bodies, the lack of political will to foster these institutions, several

---

[31] An early and important work on local self-government in the subcontinent is Hugh Tinker's *The Foundations of Local Self-Government in India, Pakistan and Burma*. Tinker, an influential early thinker on local self-governments in post-independent South Asia, was a scholar-practitioner—having served in local government in both India and England.

[32] Article 40 in the Constitution of India, under the heading 'Organisation of village panchayats', states: 'The State shall take steps to organise village panchayats and endow them with such powers and authority as may be necessary to enable them to function as units of self-government.'

> internal deficiencies in the functioning of Panchayati Raj Institutions and, above all, the lack of clarity about the concept itself have weakened the entire system.

What this meant was that mukhiyas did not draw much *formal power* from panchayati raj institutions. However, insofar as the state at the Centre could not reach them, the entrenched elite in a village drew substantial *informal power* from the intermixed hierarchies of caste, class and gender, and functioned as de facto mukhiyas.

Sudhir Mishra's modern classic *Hazaaron Khwaishein Aisi* (2005) has a scene that exemplifies this sort of informal power. A group of Naxal youth convince the exploited Dalits in a village in Bhojpur to protest against their oppressor, an upper-caste Thakur (who is presumably also the mukhiya of the village). A charged procession, shouting slogans and demanding justice, arrives at the Thakur's doorstep. The Naxal youth are ecstatic. The central character's voice-over declares: Revolution was at hand.

And suddenly, the Thakur clutches his chest and complains of a pain.

The effing landlord, the voice-over goes, *had a heart attack. The villagers who were screaming for his blood a minute ago were suddenly overcome by an ancient dutiful urge to save him.*

This 'ancient dutiful urge' was nothing but centuries' worth of ingrained caste hierarchies that granted vast powers to upper-caste landlords.

The devolution of formal power to panchayats began in 1993, when the Seventy-third Amendment to the Indian Constitution was passed. Of the many sweeping changes the amendment proposed, four stand out: first, every village (gram panchayat) had to democratically elect a headman (a mukhiya) for a period of five years; second, a fixed share of the seats were to be reserved for women and Dalits; third, a Finance Commission would be constituted that would mandate devolution of funds to panchayats; fourth, all decisions in a panchayat will be made in a participatory manner. This would be via villagers assembling in a 'gram sabha', a public meeting, and jointly deciding the direction of village development with their leaders.

In 1991, a full forty-five years after he died, Ambedkar was awarded the Bharat Ratna, the nation's highest civilian honour. Two years later, with the passing of the Seventy-third Amendment, his old rival Gandhi seemingly had his way: villages across the country swung once more towards a more formally recognised independent form of government. Still, Ambedkar's fears were acknowledged in at least two ways: first, many powers were not devolved to local governments; second, the law mandated that seats be reserved for the marginalised.

In the end, this was not a return to the 'former past' of Venkatarangaiya, one that prevailed in the ancient times, but a more moderate correction of the path local government institutions had taken since. For over 200 years, India had gone too far in one direction for the avant-garde dream of independent village republics to be a reality.

Eight years ago, I first attended a gram sabha[33] in the village of Mahant Maniyari under gloomy skies that showered and

[33] Arguably the finest modern scholar on gram sabhas is the discipline-defying economist Vijayendra Rao. (Rao—Biju to friends—and I are currently working on a set of papers on the political economy of villages in Karnataka.) Anyone interested in democratic decentralisation should read him.

prematurely ended proceedings. It was as dramatic as they came. Few other gram sabhas in Bihar's 8,400 panchayats would have been as eventful. That, however, is more of a statement on how much of a private, undemocratic affair such sabhas tend to be.

On paper, a gram sabha is a spectacular idea. It envisages a grand get-together of the entire village. The mukhiya and other local government officials put forward plans for the coming year; the villagers debate and discuss them, proposing ideas of their own. In the end, a consensus is reached and a document prepared. A path is charted, one paved by the villagers themselves. The mukhiya is merely a gatekeeper. A gram sabha is, therefore, 'the largest deliberative institution in human history'.[34]

Predictably, the asli zindagi of gram sabhas is markedly different. Often, they are a charade, a Gram Sham. In many parts of India—Bihar being no exception—the mukhiya and his team of brokers, contractors, local bureaucrats and political entities huddle together and produce a document that best fits their interests. The interests of these few are often at odds with those at the margins.

You cannot know this, of course, unless you go to a village or are told by someone in the know. The documents are perfect: the numbers add up, the counter-checks tally, the signatures are legible and legitimate. What's more, they often look like the outcome of reasonably meticulous research, having taken into consideration the opinion of a wide range of people from

---

34 P. Sanyal & V. Rao, *Oral Democracy: Deliberation in Indian Village Assemblies*, Cambridge University Press, Cambridge, 2019, p. 1. See also: V. Rao and P. Sanyal, 'Dignity through discourse: Poverty and the culture of deliberation in Indian village democracies', *The Annals of the American Academy of Political and Social Science*, 629(1), 2010, pp.146–172.

the village. However, these documents inhabit a reality all of their own.[35]

Indeed, this is a phenomenon that harks back all the way to the early British civil servants who were ordered to keep excessively precise records of an imprecise, chaotic society. Seeing no way–and realising quickly that no one really cares–the early British officers fudged their way to medals and honours.

When they left, their Indian counterparts perfected this truly dismal art.

Our party attending the gram sabha included a group of young researchers, and Ashish Ranjan, the inspirational activist from Araria who co-ran the union of unorganised workers, JJSS.

Mahant Maniyari's sabha should have been just another sham. Indeed, in the days that Sanjay Sahni was an electrician, that is what it was. Now, however, things had transformed–the mazdoors had begun to bridge the distance between themselves and the state. The gap was almost wholly eliminated when it came to the NREGA. An apathetic, deaf state had been forced to listen; would the mukhiya and his team of ward members, the panchayat's democratic face, begin to listen too?

Sanjay Sahni, who had by now fought this entrenched local elite for more than a year, did not believe so. Initially, he

---

[35] These views are echoed in R. Veeraraghavan's excellent dissertational research of 2015, studying the NREGA in Andhra Pradesh, a part of which focuses on gram sabhas. (See: *Open Governance and Surveillance: A Study of the National Rural Employment Program in Andhra Pradesh*, https://escholarship.org/uc/item/3805n440.)

> 'The gram sabha is an example of the "anti-politics machine," a ceremonial exercise at best if it actually happens, and otherwise a "failure" but a meeting on paper to conform to the rules that meetings should happen. These meetings reflect the apathy of the bureaucratic state, which seems to not be interested in adding additional work, and particularly to avoid any political backlash. But they are organized because it is mandated.'

wanted nothing to do with the gram sabha. The previous year, a thousand mazdoors had worked on various NREGA schemes in these villages, all by themselves, under the banner of their own unregistered labour union—the Bihar Manrega Watch. The BMW, as we saw in the previous chapter, ran its own parallel sabhas.

But the gram sabha, enshrined in the Seventy-third Amendment of the Constitution, was an important institution for democratic dialogue. If Sanjay and the mazdoors could fix the seemingly unrepairable NREGA system in these villages, perhaps it was time to push the envelope a little. Sanjay was hesitant, and not without reason. Politically, the mukhiya and Sanjay had reached an unspoken understanding: the NREGA was the mazdoors', the political authority the mukhiya's. All of this fell into place organically, there was no formal agreement. Over time, the mazdoors asserted themselves, and the mukhiya and his brokers had ceded ground. To have everything play out in a sabha would mean rocking a steady boat. Why bring tensions to the fore?

In the end, however, Sanjay decided to participate. He felt that, just as in the case of the NREGA, it had fallen upon Mahant Maniyari's mazdoors to be model citizens, to show the way for the rest of the state.

We got to the sabha venue—a small open space by the panchayat office—well in time. As ever, Mahant Maniyari's women mazdoors were ready and waiting. A makeshift stage was set up; chairs were arranged for the dignitaries. Sanjay and Ashish were natural candidates for occupying a pair of these chairs. The rest of us, although we were asked to accompany them, preferred to sit elsewhere. For some reason, I chose to perch on a seven-foot-high wall directly behind the stage. A few male mazdoors soon followed suit.

My vantage point allowed me a brilliant, Sanjaya-esque[36] view of the proceedings: a consultant with the World Bank, who had also come to observe, walked around with a camera in hand, steadily taking pictures; children huddled in a corner, with some brave ones even climbing up the wall I was on and peering about curiously; above, the clouds were an ominous grey, the scent of rain gripped the air; suddenly, there was a commotion in the panchayat office; and finally, the mukhiya of Mahant Maniyari walked in, files and notebooks in hand.

We got down to business without much ado. Ashish conducted the proceedings. He began by providing some context. The gram sabha, he explained, came at the end of a series of ward sabhas. A ward is the sub-unit of a gram panchayat, each represented by an elected ward member. Ward sabhas are mini-gram sabhas. Here, men and women met with their respective ward members (colloquially referred to as ward 'numbers') and proposed NREGA projects. Some mazdoors wanted to build roads, others canals, still others drains and so on. The ward members noted all these ideas down in their notebooks. Not every project could be undertaken in a single financial year. Thus, it fell upon the gram sabha to choose between the various ward projects by a voice-vote.

The mukhiya rose and read out from the list of proposed projects for the first ward. The responses came in the form of cheers, grunts or silences. Very soon, we ran into problems: we did not have mazdoors from all the wards present at the sabha. Therefore, the mukhiya would read out a whole list of projects from a ward—say, the third—and no one would have an opinion on any of these.

---

36 Sanjaya, of the Mahabharata, had been blessed with the ability to view the Kurukshetra war panoramically, which helped him to narrate the events as they were taking place to the blind king Dhritarashtra.

Things, however, took an exciting turn when we came across a ward which had a fair representation in the audience. However, those present were confronted with a list of projects they had never seen before. Every named project was met with opposition. The ward member grew restive. Clearly, this was a list generated out of thin air, not through a ward sabha. Instead of pointing this out (and thus be forced to turn instigator himself), Ashish pretended like he did not understand. He chided the mazdoors for proposing a list of works in the ward sabha and then summarily rejecting all of them in the gram sabha. The mazdoors retorted by saying that there had never been a ward sabha.

The ward member panicked, the mukhiya stuttered, the mazdoors roared.

It began to drizzle.

Seizing his chance, the concerned ward member, a short, moustached man who could have been an extra in a movie, made a dash for the stage. He let out an incoherent stream of words. No one really knew how to react, and for a few crystal moments, we simply watched.

Suddenly, he grabbed the notebook off the mukhiya's hands and left.

By now, the rain was steadily pounding down, the mood had turned sombre, the proceedings distracted. The mukhiya hastened the end, citing rain.

Had Gandhi and Ambedkar watched the sabha at Mahant Maniyari, they would have both returned home smiling.

For Babasaheb, this would have been a confirmation of

his beliefs a full sixty-five years after he espoused them. This sabha at Maniyari had a battery of facilitators–Ashish and the rest of us–to ensure effective proceedings. Yet, we had nothing to show for it. Our best achievement was to reinforce a sorry truism: elected representatives are corrupt and narrow-minded. What else but parochialism and ignorance could result in these leaders being repeatedly elected?

The Mahatma would have pointed out that the sabha comprised more women than men. More jatis than you could count on your fingers. More Dalits than upper castes questioning their leaders. Hindus and Muslims roared as one when confronted with farzi lists of projects. Granted, this was an unusual village. And yes, we had no reasoned debate on anything, no people's plan chalked out. But the significance of the Sabha, the Mahatma would say, lay beyond mere outcomes; it was living proof of how far we had come as a people and of the immense potential at hand. This was India, his India–their India–diverse but unquestionably democratic, lumbering but moving forward.[37]

---

[37] For a much richer characterisation—and a much more formal treatment—of gram sabhas, see: P. Sanyal & V. Rao, *Oral Democracy: Deliberation in Indian Village Assemblies*, Cambridge University Press, Cambridge, 2019. Analysing transcripts of 298 gram sabhas held across four southern states (Kerala, Karnataka, the erstwhile Andhra Pradesh and Tamil Nadu), the authors argue that, inter alia, these sabhas emerge as crucial forums for marginalised groups to articulate their demands. They note that:

> 'Low-caste citizens, who may hesitate to say some things in social settings, are less hesitant to say them in the gram sabha knowing that they are engaging in a kind of political performance. Politicians, in their turn, engage in a different kind of political performance in which they try to appear to be responsive to citizens, and try to avoid expressing the kind of quotidian prejudice that would turn away potential voters.'

Over the years, I have met many mukhiyas and they seem to come, like all of us, in many shapes and forms: some, like the mukhiya from a village nestled in the hills by the Indo-Nepal border, betray a sense of disinterest, almost boredom, in their work; others are young and enthusiastic, unafraid to speak of the compromises they have made while in power; still others, like Vinod Bhaiya in Buxar, with whom I had many fruitful conversations about policy, are thoughtful.[38]

However, there are also many that fit the dabang mukhiya or (the now less commonly used) Bolero mukhiya stereotypes—descriptor-prefixes that capture the essence of what these characters are like. Much like Salman Khan in the blockbuster movie of that name, they are dabang. In popular parlance, 'dabang' refers to a person who is authoritative, overpowering, fearless, even dictatorial. They are also the village elites, and a decade ago were often found travelling in Mahindra Boleros, a seven-seater SUV that is best suited to the ups and downs of rough village roads. More importantly, Boleros were status symbols, costing upwards of Rs 7 lakh, and given their sizes, could hold up to eight henchmen.

Of all my meetings with mukhiyas, one stands out, not for what transpired, but for who it was with.

On 2 October 2012, I met, for the first and only time, the mukhiya of Ratnauli, Raj Kumar Sahni.

It was on the same day we attended the gram sabha at Mahant Maniyari. I do not know why we went to the Sahnis' house for

---

[38] The late Shaibal Gupta's 2001 *Economic and Political Weekly* piece on panchayat elections in Bihar offers a nice starting point for anyone looking at panchayats and mukhiyas in the twenty-first century. Gupta, who ran Asian Development Research Institute (ADRI) with great distinction for many years, is considered to be among the finest social scientists in Bihar in recent years. See: Shaibal Gupta, 'New Panchayats and Subaltern Resurgence', *Economic and Political Weekly*, Vol. 36, No. 29, 2001, pp. 2742–2744.

tea. Do not get me wrong: he had invited us. However, while the murder of Ram Kumar Thakur was a few months in the future, we had already known—thanks to Sanjay Sahni's painstaking exposé—that the mukhiya was a contemptible swindler and a thug in power.

While it would be easy to imbue the memory of the meeting with ominous signs, the truth is that it felt very ordinary. The man did not wear a snake around his neck and his house was nondescript, barely distinguishable from any other relatively wealthy man's house in the village. The conversation was civil, if awkward. We had sugary tea and made small talk; we skirted any contentious topic and left.

A combination of how the people's movement grew in Ratnauli and fate's mysterious ways ensured our paths never crossed again.

3

From Darkness to Fight

We were at NaREGA Chowk, Sanjay's adda. It was here that, armed with hundreds of printouts, a loudspeaker and a videographer, Sanjay first went about exposing corruption. Now, many months later, on a day when winter made shy advances, he was mobiliser and teacher, making fiery proclamations and didactic pronouncements. The crowd spilt over from the chowk onto the streets. The BMW had become popular in these parts.

Sanjay and Ani–who consulted with the government of Bihar on rural development issues back then–did most of the talking. I was free to observe and make small talk with whomever I wished. I sat by a woman in a green sari, her deep brown eyes shining in the afternoon sun, and asked about the beedi she was smoking. She said she had to smoke, otherwise her stomach would balloon: *pet phool jaata hai.*

There was another woman who had come from Rampur Mani, a panchayat that had only recently seen members join BMW. She had heard of Sanjay and his collective of pioneering mazdoors. As Ani listed the basics of demanding and undertaking work–'always keep your job card with you'; 'make sure you know the minimum wage'–the woman from Rampur Mani listened, attentive. She was thin but, like every woman mazdoor, sturdy.

The questions from the crowd flew thick and fast at Sanjay and Ani. There were two types of members in the crowd: those who wanted work and those who, having worked, wanted their money. The latter had usually been tricked into working on the NREGA by their mukhiya with the promise of money.

The two men responding to them could best be described as a live helpline: question followed answer followed question.

Soon, it was the Rampur Mani woman's turn. Her problem fell in the latter category.

'When did you work?' we asked.

'A few years ago.'

This was worrying; the more recent the non-payment, the higher the likelihood of recovery. If she were playing chess, she'd have lost her knights by now.

'How many years ago?'

'Maybe two or three.'

'And you haven't been paid anything?' Ani asked.

'No,' the woman responded.

'Nothing at all?'

'No.'

The rooks, the bishops, all gone.

'What did you work on?'

'Some road-work.'

'What road-work?'

'Some.'

'Do you have a job card?'

The job card was crucial—the queen in terms of chance of payment—a document that recorded how much she had worked, where she had worked and how much money was rightfully earned.

She nodded her head.

'No?' Ani asked.

'What is a job card?' she asked slowly.

'A card–it's got your photo on it.'

'He took it away.'

'Who?'

'He.'

'Who is he? The mukhiya?'

'No.'

'The mate? The broker?'

'Yes, maybe.'

'How many days did you work?'

'100'

'A 100 days and you haven't been paid?'

'Yes.'

'How could you allow that?'

Silence.

'Do you know how much you are due?' Ani asked.

'Yes,' she said, and added softly, '10,000.'

'14,400!' Ani corrected her and asked: 'How can you not have a single document to prove you are owed that money? You are owed 14,400 rupees from a few years ago–there is no record of it. Who will give it to you? Why will anyone listen to you? Where is the proof?'

The woman was silent. Suddenly, she began to weep. Her woes tumbled out. She was a widow. She had young children; she wanted them to go to school, to become somebody. She needed the money.

While I watched Ani put an arm around her and console her, I realised that the woman may have already known what we had told her. She must have been resigned to her fate. And then, she must have heard of Ratnauli and Mahant Maniyari, the BMW and the incredible stories of labourers demanding and being paid, months, years after they had worked and had given up.

Perhaps the sight, earlier in the morning, of these mazdoors–so unlike any other she had seen before, belligerent, lively and demanding–further encouraged her. Perhaps the presence of us outsiders from faraway Patna may have convinced her that she had more than a slim chance. The snatched promise of a miracle may well have been harder to stomach than the certainty of daily disappointments.

It rained and we were forced to make a beeline for Damodar Paswan's hut by the chaiwallah's. Sanjay ordered a round of tea and took it upon himself to lighten the mood. He suggested we sing a song, and picked one himself. If he wanted to spread cheer, Sanjay could have done better. The song went:

Nyay naam ka cheez nahin
Anyaay badhta jaaye re
Mehnat karta dhoti waala
Topi waala khaaye re.
(There is no such thing as justice
Injustice keeps rising
The dhoti-wallah works hard
The topi-wallah eats.)

As Sanjay sang and we repeated, I found myself looking for her. She was in a corner, clinging to a pole and staring at the steadily pounding rain, soundlessly mouthing the words.

From the outside (and probably my own description so far), one might garner the impression that a people's movement is like a T20 game, filled with massive crowds and exciting, constant drama. In reality, what fuels a people's movement in twenty-first-century Bihar is what drives a test match: the humdrum of repeated patterns. Like test cricket, a movement usually involves a few frenzied passages interspersed by long spells of repetitive, but often riveting, routine. The routine builds the base for the magical.

But what does a regular day inside a people's movement look like?

In July 2015, I spent some time in Ratnauli and kept detailed notes of my stint there. Here, I reproduce snapshots from these field notes–lightly edited for clarity–covering a three-day period.

Ratnauli, 21 July, field notes

These events take place in the BMW's old 'office', a room in an unfinished brick house. Ram Babu, the owner of the house, was away in Punjab a lot those days and was kind enough to allow BMW to function out of a room there.

The office has unpainted brick walls, a tiny window and mud floors, three plastic chairs, a wooden table, an explosion of wires and papers everywhere.

My nights are spent sleeping on the charpoy outside, under skies partitioned into small diamonds by the mosquito net, until Dukha-ji, Ram Babu's grey-haired father, wakes me up with a rousing 'Jai Shri Ram'. At 4 a.m. This wake-up call–when the skies are still black, with the odd traversing star the only light up there–is timed to ensure we perform our morning ablutions in open fields under the bum-saving invisibility of the darkness.

In the morning, after naashta, two women walk into the office, asking for Sanjay. They want Sanjay to look something up on the internet. They claim to have been paid less than they should have got–in fact, they have only been paid for half the days. Sanjay fires up his laptop and checks the NREGA website. He tallies records. He asks them for their passbook. He deduces that they have actually been paid in two separate spells–one-half each time. He tells them to go back to the bank and update their passbooks: 'the money will be there', he confidently asserts.

I ask the women what it is the 'internet' does: they explain that it has all the information they require regarding the NREGA. If any of the records are wrong, they would go to the block office and get it fixed.

Meanwhile, Gobind Sah walks in asking for Sanjay. He is perhaps the oldest man in the village (eighty to ninety years by his own estimate). He can barely see: his eyes are clouded over. Gobind Sah's wife is long deceased. He had a daughter who died aged one. This is his sasural, his wife's village. Sah tells Sanjay he didn't get his BPL (Below Poverty Line) card. New cards have been distributed under the National Food Security Act (NFSA). Gobind Sah says he has been wrongly excluded.

A discussion about his pensions follow: he is entitled to Rs 400 per month. He is usually paid in lump sums–Rs 1,200 per three months. Sanjay says he will think over both issues and revert with the correct strategy.

Meeting of local members of BMW.

Participants: Madina Begum, Sushila Devi, Basmati Devi, Somariya Devi, Shakuntala Devi, Leela Devi, Savitri Devi, Phulkawali Devi, Chandrakala Devi, Bindushree Devi, Ram Lal Devi, Sudha Devi, Dharamshila Devi, Mukhiya Devi, Vandushree Devi, Paso Devi, Jamila Khatun, Reena Devi, Lalpa Devi, Raj Mahal Sahni, Rajender Sah.

All participants from Mahant Maniyari Village, Ratnauli Panchayat.

Before the meeting, a discussion ensues about Mahesh Sah between the women saathis–led by Chandrakala Devi–and Sanjay. Mahesh Sah stays in one of the houses by NaREGA

Chowk. He had employed some women to harvest grain with the promise of paying them by giving them a share of the harvest. Unfortunately, because of the rain, the grain was spoiled. The women claim it was 'fit only to be eaten by animals'. Sah argued that since it was the very same grain that had been promised, the women must accept it, whatever the quality provided. The women protested and refused to accept any payment at all, except in the form of fresh grain. As of the time of the meeting, the two parties had reached a stalemate.

The meeting begins. First, Sanjay begins to examine a 'Register' of members from Ward No. 5. This is in the form of a simple ruled long notebook. Starting with the third page of the register, we have the following columns:

Name	Father's/Husband's name	Mobile Number

Sanjay chastises the women for not maintaining the register properly. There are several mobile numbers missing. None of the women from Ward No. 5 can write, a fact known to all in the room, except me. The women blame Subodh (a co-resident in the ward who can write) whose job it was to fill the register. Sanjay responds: '*Hum kyon nahin likhwaate? Sabke ghar mein bacche nahin hai?*' (Why can't we get it written ourselves? Can't you get your children involved?)

By 2015, the collective–or, to use the local term, sangathan–no longer worked on only the NREGA. This was even reflected in a new name. While BMW still existed, a new sangathan was formed, its nomenclature reflecting the group's deep roots in Indian people's movements of the past. Like that pioneering people's movement in Rajasthan, MKSS, this unregistered labour union was called the Samaj Parivartan Shakti Sangathan, or SPSS.

A discussion on ration cards follows.

It is revealed that the PDS dealer distributes rations only covering seven to eight months in the year. This year is a particularly bad one, given that the government has issued new ration cards in line with the recently passed National Food Security Act.

The NFSA, enacted in Parliament in late 2013, had expanded benefits to a broader cross-section of individuals: nearly three-quarters of Indians living in villages were entitled to rations now. While this was great news, the transition from the old system to the new one could be painful: new ration cards had to be issued and the actual entitlements were often hazy, allowing for middle-men and corrupt ration dealers to exploit misinformation to their advantage.[39]

Sanjay, after listening to a spate of complaints about irregular ration distribution, makes a few brief points about how to fight for rations. Here are some excerpts:

'*Halla karke baarah le sakte hain; 200 saal se log sochte rahein. Sochne se kuchh nahin milta.*' (If we make noise, we will get rations for all twelve months. People have been thinking and dreaming of these things for the past 200 years. Nothing ever happens through just thinking.)

If you want ration every month, Sanjay goes on, you have to work hard. You have to talk to the supplier and ask him if he has sent the 'maal' (rations) to the local dealer. If yes, then pressurise the dealer—'*dharna karke le sakte hain*' (we can strike). If not, one can pressurise the supplier too.

Sanjay then comes up with a simple motto: '*Har mahine tel lao; Har mahine ration lao.*' (Get kerosene every month, get ration every month.)

Towards the end, Sanjay is more aggressive: '*Log darte hain,*' he says. '*Ye sochte hain ki agar hum marte hain, to bacchon ka kya*

---

[39] For more on the NFSA and issues around it, see the Right to Food Campaign website: http://www.righttofoodcampaign.in/.

hoga?' (People are scared [of protesting for their rights]—they think that if we die, what will become of the kids?)

But that is not the right attitude, he says: 'We are many, we cannot be harmed. And even if some of us are, we are too many to be wiped out.'

Unemployment benefits under the NREGA is the topic that is taken up next. This is a tricky subject since, even though the Act mandates that everyone should be given unemployment benefits if they are denied work by the state, no one in the country actually avails these benefits. But the mazdoors of Manrega Watch are not to be reined in by empirical impossibilities.

Citing the law, a group of mazdoors had filed a request with the block development officer a couple of weeks ago. There has been no response thus far.

Sanjay talks of writing to the local MLA. With the elections coming up (recently announced for October–November), Sanjay believes the time is ripe for protest.

'*Ab teen mahine baad jab aayega vote maangne, tab bol sakte hain ... Ab dharna mein baithenge to bahut chance hai.*' (In three months, he will come asking for votes. Then we can tell him of our woes. Our chances of success are good if we go on a strike now.)

Ratnauli, 22 July, field notes

In the morning, we go to Ratnauli. Sanjay has to meet his mother, who lives by herself (his father is in Delhi, managing Sanjay's electrician-khokha for him). I briefly catch Sanjay writing a letter. I don't ask him what it is. He seems to want to have it delivered to somebody. Eventually, after some frantic phone coordination, the letter is placed with Santosh (an upper-caste, educated youth who briefly functioned as Sanjay's right-hand) who is to give it to the persons concerned.

We lose the morning to doing nothing. Sanjay's creaky old motorcycle tends to break down every now and then, and he is wary of taking it anywhere for fear that it might stop again midway. Our original plan was to go to a panchayat where the movement is still at a nascent stage.

However, we spend much of the morning at Ratnauli Chowk, watching the rain and children at the local school as Sanjay and his cousin (who runs a kirana shop) try their best to get the motorcycle up and running.

In the afternoon, we return to Mahant Maniyari. On our way, we walk past an old man. He is clad in a clean white vest, a white dhoti. His grey hair is neatly kept, and his beard is almost regal. He uses a stick to walk slowly. I ask Sanjay who he is. '*Hoga, koi oonch jati ka*,' he responds. (He must be someone from a high caste.)

The contrast with the semi-blind Govind Sah from the previous day could not be starker.

At 2 p.m., under a blazing sun, things are slow, and I decide the time is ripe for a bath. I gather my towel, soap and mug. I crank the hand-pump and fill up the bucket. The hand pump is by the buffalo shed, right in front of the office. Somewhat self-consciously, I strip down to my boxers and, with a quick glance to make sure no one is around, begin.

Soon, I notice a goat has ambled into the scene and is eyeing—I think—my soap. I move the soap away from its field of vision.

I then turn left to see a group of fifteen or so women walk in a file to the office. Seeing that Sanjay has briefly stepped out, they wait outside the office, settling down on the charpoy and around. I feel like a spectacle, with thirty-two eyes (thirty human, two goat) on me. The women, many of whom are facing me, are quiet. I decide it would be bizarre to acknowledge their presence, so I entirely avert my eyes. I hasten to finish, praying that they have more important things on their minds.

All such hopes are dashed when one of them rushes to refill my bucket just as I scoop the last mug of water from it. Not only were they watching, I realise, but so intent was their study of my bathing technique that even the water-levels in my bucket were being monitored.

Sanjay arrives—far too late to save me any embarrassment—and the women proceed indoors. When I am bathed and clothed, I go into the office myself. I am told that the women were from a neighbouring hamlet: they had come to show Sanjay the NREGA job cards they had recently been given. He scrutinises and approves every one of the job cards, and shoots off a few instructions on how to handle them (Never lose them and never give them to anyone, especially the mukhiya). The women are relieved to be told that the documents are original and take his leave.

A little while later, two more women—Mandesri Devi and another saathi—come to the office. It is 3 p.m. They explain that they went to the block office to hand over a letter (the same one Sanjay was writing) and got a 'receiving'.

(Much before verbification of nouns became popular [Google], the Indian bureaucracy nounified verbs. 'Receiving' is one of those words, standing for an official chit of paper that is passed on to a citizen acknowledging that a request has been made of the state.)

I ask the two women if they have read the letter Sanjay sent with them. They have not. This is because they cannot read. I ask them if they know what the letter says. I paraphrase Mandesri Devi's response:

> We demanded payment of unemployment benefits because we haven't got it. Now we have given you sufficient time to process the payments, and because you haven't responded, we'll sit on a dharna within a week if you don't respond.

I turn to Sanjay and he says that is exactly what the letter said.

Mandesri Devi explains what happened at the block office. First, the programme officer–the man in charge of NREGA for the entire block–refused to accept the letter. Then, when they insisted, he threw the letter back at them. Eventually, seeing that these women refused to go away, the block engineer accepted the letter. He then gave them the receiving acknowledging it. The receiving is genuine, Sanjay confirms.

In the evening, before twilight inspires woozy revelry from the dancing fireflies, Sanjay and I watch kids (Dukha-ji's grandchildren) play a 'tractor' game: they pretend that a strange contraption that has a handlebar of sorts and a wheel is a tractor and run around ploughing the earth outside our office.

Ratnauli, 23 July, field notes

Meeting.

Members present: Lakhi Devi, Ram Kali Devi, Suhag Devi, Santi Devi, Sunaina Devi, Saraswat Devi, Subhiya Devi, Gulla Devi.

We are in the office. Lakhi Devi sits at the front of the small group, on a blue tarpaulin that's been laid out on the muddy floor. She clearly lords over–in a small way–the rest.[40] A long tilak streaks the parting in her hair a deep red. Sanjay sits down on the tarpaulin too, facing this group.

The meeting starts with introductions, or 'parichay'. Sanjay starts with describing why parichay is important. One must be

---

[40] Lakhi Devi went on to contest the next panchayat elections. She became sarpanch of her panchayat in 2016.

conscious of who one is. Not just enough to say I am so-and-so's wife or daughter. It is important to say one's own name, one's occupation and whether one belongs to an organisation.

Lakhi Devi goes first. She says her name; she says she belongs to SPSS and talks of her 'haq', rights.

Gulla Devi is up next. She introduces herself and then says that she belongs to a sangathan called 'Narega'.

Sanjay is annoyed: '*Naam yaad nahin hai to chhod do.*' (If you don't remember the name, then don't bother.)

She knows what she wants to do though: '*Didi log ke saath rehte hain; haq ke liye ladte hain.*' (We are with our sisters; we fight for our rights.)

Sanjay gets her to repeat the name of the sangathan. She trips up at Parivartan. Every single time.

Shanti Devi, who has a lovely round blue bindi to go with her blue sari, gives a fine introduction.

Sanjay says she speaks too softly.

Leelam Devi: '*Didi bhaiya sab judke kaam karte hain; ladai karte hain.*' (We join with our brother and sisters and work; we fight.)

Sanjay then explains how the name 'Samaj Parivartan Shakti Sangathan' can be shortened to 'SPSS', so everyone can remember.

In my opinion, that is confusing too.

Sanjay moves on to articulating his new vision for the sangathan. He begins with articulating SPSS's thinking. ('*SPSS ka soch kya hai?*')

(When he says 'SPSS'—a whispered ripple floats through the room, everyone is practising!)

Sanjay says he alone cannot bring about all change.

'*SPSS office ke andar nahin hai; is Maniyari mein nahin hai; SPSS har admi aur har aurat mein hai, har aadmi aur har aurat ka hai.*'

(SPSS is not inside this office; it is not in Maniyari; SPSS is in every man and woman and is of every man and woman.)

Sanjay lays out the new strategy—think small, think local, help one district, 100 villages. This is a campaign he later christens: 'Small Is Beautiful'.

Sunaina Devi is nodding off.

Sanjay explains: '*Kabhi-kabhi so jaate hain log meeting mein.*' (People sometimes sleep during the meeting.) He gently tosses his mobile phone—hardy, Nokia, non-smart, basic model—in her direction.

It lands a few inches away from her, she wakes up with a start to giggles all round.

In the year 1973, a little girl from the village of Reni near the Tibet border spied a group of lumbermen walking towards the forest near her village. She rushed to Gaura Devi, the head of the village Mahila Mandal (Women's Group), and informed her of what she saw. Sensing trouble, Gaura Devi banded together a group of housewives in her village and went into the forest. Together, the women confronted the lumbermen, pleading with them to not cut the trees. The forest, the women explained, was theirs. The men first abused, then threatened the women. The women, resolute, refused to budge. The men were eventually forced to retire.

This incident marked the exact moment the Chipko movement came into its own as 'a peasant movement in defence of traditional forest rights'.

About 1,300 kilometres, a full twenty-four-hour drive and three decades separate the protestors at Reni from those at Ratnauli. However, they share two similarities: first, in both instances, these were peasants fighting the state and demanding what was rightfully theirs; second–even more so in Ratnauli than in Reni–women played a starring role in sparking and sustaining the movement.

Why have women dominated these people's movements? A combination of how the NREGA works and the structure of Indian society offers one explanation. In a 2014 talk in Bangalore, Sanjay explained: 'If a husband and wife both work as NREGA mazdoors, then they may die of hunger because the money only comes after a six-month delay. What will the family do during the wait?'[41]

The NREGA does not discriminate between men and women at work. By law, everyone gets paid the same. However, the private market for casual labour pays men more than women. Further, the more enterprising–or desperate or privileged–among men can travel to Patna or Delhi or Punjab or Kerala for work, an option almost entirely unavailable to women. Thus, one reason more women collectivise around an NREGA movement is because of the higher opportunity costs of working on the NREGA for men.[42]

[41] He was speaking at the 'Re-wiring Women's Rights Debates in the Digital Age' short course organised by IT for Change, Bengaluru, 13 September 2014.

[42] Using data from the National Sample Survey (2011–12), Sudha Narayanan and Upasak Das argue that NREGA has performed 'reasonably well' in terms of providing employment for women, but that women from Bihar demand very little work (about one-fifth of the national rate) and are disproportionately denied work too. The data comes from a time before the Muzaffarpur movement. However, given the considerable demand for work and participation in the movement, the fact remains that there exists large latent demand for work among women—especially when faced with a responsive state—that is not being captured in conventional surveys. See: Narayanan, Sudha and Das, Upasak, 'Women Participation and Rationing in the Employment Guarantee Scheme', *Economic and Political Weekly*, Vol. 49, No. 46, 2014, pp. 46–53.

I have had the privilege of meeting several women who have worked with—and sometimes *around*—BMW/SPSS. In the early days, there was Krishna Devi from Ratnauli, quiet and large-eyed, tirelessly managing the day-to-day affairs of the sangathan. She had to stop working when her husband grew jealous of her rising prominence and threatened to swallow poison if she did not return to her old life.

Subsequently, there was Reena Devi, perhaps the brightest and most efficient of them all. At some point, she was so influential that the mukhiya co-opted her into conning some mazdoors into working on a long-shelved project. Predictably, the payments never came. The mazdoors, and later Reena Devi herself, returned to the sangathan.

Then there was Somariya Devi, grey-haired and spunky, who often sent meals up to the old office. As dusk fell, she would fire up her hookah and perch, rather regally, on the charpoy and entertain us with her many stories.

And finally, the pair who, to my mind, most singularly represent the women of the sangathan: the stoic and passionate Medina Begum and the fiery, high-pitched Mandesri Devi.

I have seen them at the forefront of protests, their fists clenched in solidarity, their voices sloganeering in unison, unabashed, unafraid, passionate.

On a sweltering day in 2017, I found myself in a conference room in Patna's Old Secretariat building. At the meeting, there were two warring sides, both from Muzaffarpur: the first was a clutch of the SPSS's women mazdoors, accompanied by Sanjay Sahni; the second comprised a virtual ladder of officials, descending downwards from the director of the District Rural Development

Authority of Muzaffarpur to the PRS of Mahant Maniyari. The issue was a wage dispute between the mazdoors and the officials. The secretary of the Rural Development Department was acting as mediator.

Accusations flew thick and fast, each side growing more agitated. The secretary expressed that he was both astonished and proud of the extraordinary argumentative abilities of the women mazdoors. The saathis were indeed typically forceful and articulate that day. They guffawed when officials misrepresented facts; they defended their positions from a place of obvious familiarity with the intricacies of the NREGA law. When the lies of the local officials got too severe, they appealed to the secretary's sense of inherent justice, their voices choking.

In the afternoon, as all the back and forth threatened to end in a stalemate, the secretary excused himself and left the room. We were all allowed a breather. One by one, the other officials left, for a quick cup of tea or to relieve themselves.

I then noticed that the women mazdoors had suddenly quietened and were crouched in a semi-huddle in a corner.

Had all that arguing drained them?

I inched closer to see if all was okay. By virtue of my superior height (strictly average anywhere but among the women of rural Bihar), I was able to see past their bent heads and noticed that they were peering at an image on a smartphone screen.

Medina Begum's two fingers—which had perhaps never held a pen—effortlessly pinched the screen and separated. The image zoomed in on to a young woman's face.

Achhi hai, someone declared. *She's nice*. A murmur of assents followed.

It was a picture of her future daughter-in-law.

This scene, to my mind, captured something of the essence of the Ratnauli movement.

Here they were, a group of the most marginalised members of Bihari society, in a world being transformed by technology, sitting in a magnificent colonial structure—that symbolised at once both grandeur and apathy, and was the very heart of the state government—fighting for their rights with nothing but the strength of their collective will and their combined intelligence.

And doing all this while never quite losing their sense of excitement about the other things in life, big and small.

The innovative use of everyday technology has been central to the spread of the movement.

There was a time when nearly every other day my phone would ring, and I would hear the greeting 'saathi' in a grave (bordering on morose) tone. The voice was Sanjay's. This would be followed by pre-recorded messages on a range of topics: for instance, an announcement that the NREGA wages had been credited into labourer accounts in the panchayat of Dumri; an update on the ongoing strike at the district collector's office; an anomaly noticed in pension payments this season; the transfer of a key local official.

I was one of a few thousand who received these calls. Of course, I was not the target audience, but a privileged eavesdropper. The messages, brought to thousands of mazdoors of the movement by the digital platform *awaaz.de*, were instrumental in keeping the movement alive and building a sense of community in the early years. As Sanjay once said: 'You call once, and 500–5,000 persons will benefit, in one minute!'[43]

[43] Quoted from Sanjay Sahni's interview on the TV show *Satyamev Jayate*. See: https://www.youtube.com/watch?v=HnrdEPIWyOs.

Automated mass calling may have existed three decades ago, but what makes the movement a uniquely twenty-first-century enterprise is the starring role the internet plays. It was of course Sanjay's chance tryst with the internet that set off a chain of improbable events, birthing a movement. Since then, the internet has continuously empowered Sanjay and the mazdoors. He is now an expert at navigating the contours of various government websites, and this is what gives the movement its edge. Here is Sanjay once more: 'Many women in the movement are illiterate, but their faith in the computer is supreme ... I have seen them threaten officials of the government saying, *if you are lying, I will have all this checked on the computer.*'[44]

The advent of smartphones–and WhatsApp–has further embedded technology in the movement. Workers use WhatsApp to coordinate work and strikes. Mazdoors who can barely write their own names diligently take photographs and videos as proof of working on NREGA worksites. These come in handy when they are accused of shirking by government officials or when records are falsified and payments are denied.

The internet has also helped build bridges, in large and small ways. Sanjay and I were once visiting Kanti Devi's village, Agha Nagar. Kanti, who had over the past year become a reliable presence in the SPSS office, had made hundreds of trips to Ratnauli. But this was Sanjay's first trip to Agha Nagar. As we readied the clearing for a meeting in front of her house, laying chairs and sheets by a grunting buffalo chewing the cud, a young man with a mobile phone walked out of Kanti Devi's house and approached Sanjay. They exchanged warm smiles and the man introduced himself as Kanti's husband. '*Haan*,' Sanjay said, '*WhatsApp pe dekha photo aapka*.' (Yes, I saw a photo of you on WhatsApp.)

---

[44] This is also from the *Satyamev Jayate* interview.

4

A Division of Labourers[45]

Harshankar Maniyari, 2013

Sanjay Sahni has been invited to Harshankar Maniyari for a wedding in the hamlet. He is not family, nor are they—the villagers and he—friends. But the seventy-odd families in the

[45] This phrase is taken from Dr B.R. Ambedkar's famous 1944 essay 'The Annihilation of Caste' (accessed here: https://ccnmtl.columbia.edu/projects/mmt/ambedkar/web/readings/aoc_print_2004.pdf).

The full quote reads:

> '*[T]he Caste System is not merely a division of labour. It is also a division of labourers. Civilized society undoubtedly needs division of labour. But in no civilized society is division of labour accompanied by this unnatural division of labourers into watertight compartments. The Caste System is not merely a division of labourers which is quite different from division of labour—it is a hierarchy in which the divisions of labourers are graded one above the other. In no other country is the division of labour accompanied by this gradation of labourers.*'

Any understanding of the Dalit question must begin with Ambedkar. Valerian Rodrigues's *The Essential Writings of B.R. Ambedkar* remains a fine window into an extraordinary mind. Over the years, several scholars—both Dalit and others—have produced perceptive and powerful writings on the caste question. Some excellent recent works include the writings of Surinder S. Jodhka, Suraj Yengde, Ashwini Deshpande and Sujata Gidla. D.R. Nagaraj's *The Flaming Feet and Other Essays: The Dalit Movement in India* is a favourite.

hamlet owe him and the SPSS a great deal: for over two years now, most households there have been obtaining work under the NREGA, averaging nearly eighty days per year (very close to the maximum of 100) and earn a total of nearly Rs 25,000. This is no small amount. For some households, it is a near doubling of their annual income.

Sanjay asks me if I want to come for the wedding. I readily agree. Before we leave, in the elemental Maniyari darkness, a discussion ensues on the subject of our impending departure. Some women tell Sanjay not to take his motorbike. He responds, somewhat tersely: 'How can I? It doesn't even have a working headlight.' There is a subtext to the conversation. Sanjay has challenged too many people, ruffled too many feathers to be travelling by himself in the night.

We phone Navin, who is not yet a daily drunk, and ask him to take us in his auto.[46] Before long, we are on our way, the headlight throwing an island of shaky light into an ocean of darkness. On the way, Sanjay tells me we are going to a hamlet of Musahars.

Musahars are often called 'the Dalits among Dalits'. The word 'musahar' literally translates to 'the one who eats rats'.[47] To this day, they are mostly farm labour in Bihar and are severely discriminated against.[48] The Musahars of Harshankar

---

[46] Navin's alcohol intake rose to incapacitate him in the coming months. The alcohol ban of 2016 briefly brought him to his senses, but Sanjay tells me he is drinking heavily once more.

[47] 'Musa' means 'mouse', and the similarity between the two words is not incidental. Both words—*musa* and *mouse*—have the same Indo-European root *mus*, which means mouse. 'Aahar' translates to 'food'. The conjugation 'musahar', therefore, is often translated to 'rat-eaters'. Musahars are not the only caste groups in Bihar to eat rats, but the stigma of rat-eating sticks to them by virtue of their name.

[48] In his essay on the culture of Musahars, Arun Kumar notes: 'A musahar inherits and lives in a world that appears to have posed serious challenges

Maniyari all carry the title 'Manjhi'. There is no way I could have known then that another who shares their surname, the quiet and nondescript Jitan Ram Manjhi, would become the next chief minister (CM) of Bihar.

We reach the village and are welcomed like celebrities: a pair of plastic chairs are produced; stale, warm Coke is hastily served in steel tumblers; kids—their hair streaked gold and blonde by dirt and undernourishment—peer at us curiously from behind their parents' hips; the men of the house make enthusiastic small talk.

A shamiana is put up. The few 100-watt bulbs are clearly out of their depth. In the back, amidst a haze of smoke, a few cooks work with huge vessels.

Soon, we squat for dinner on three sides of a rectangular area that is slightly sunken. Plates and glasses are produced and placed before us. I make to sit with my legs folded in the padmasana style, as we usually did during ele-oota (banana-leaf meals) back home but realise that everyone else chooses to squat on their haunches. Not wanting to break tradition, I follow suit. Just like in the Western world, our eating and excreting positions now embody a certain symmetry.

Food involves lots of rice and dal and a sabzi with aloo. To my taste buds, the food we eat back at the office, mostly cooked

---

to agencies of development and hope. From abject poverty to near-zero literacy, from regular consumption of liquor to baffling complacency if they had enough for the day, from being amazingly benign to extremely unpredictable and short-tempered, from being docile, due to generations of bondage, to providing the backbone of the militant movements of the Ultra Left in the region, from child marriage to having "many" children, from yearning for a home to possessing the nature of a wanderer, the list is long. A musahar is said to inhabit a world of contradictions and extremes.' See: Kumar, Arun, 'Culture, Development and the Cultural Capital of Farce', *Economic and Political Weekly*, Vol. 41, No. 40, 2006, pp. 4281-4285+4287-4291.

by the (relatively higher-caste) Sahni women, is richer in flavour. Here, the dal is thin, the sabzi bland, I can scarcely believe we are at a wedding. (Recently, Sanjay and I reminisced about the meal, and he disagreed. He thought the food at the wedding was better than what we ate at the office.)

Once food is done, Sanjay begins to grow fidgety. The baraat has not arrived, but he insists we leave. Sita Devi and Poonam Devi, both central to the SPSS story in the village, entreat Sanjay to meet the brides (who are sisters) and bless them. He agrees, somewhat reluctantly.

We walk into the house, past low doors and small drains to an open courtyard that boasts a striking mandap straight out of a hallucinatory drug experience. The pillars are wrapped with blue and golden paper; ornate plastic flowers hang from the top; party lights wind their way around everything like trippy creepers in shades of pink and blue and fluorescent greens; below, the bare floor is adorned by a rangoli of concentric circles made of coloured petals; a man in a cap—the local wedding planner, perhaps—is painting streaks of jhatak pink on the floor around the mandap.

I am brought out of my colourful reverie by the sight of the shy brides. The older one is smiling, her sister seems oddly... lost. Their mothers and aunts crowd around us, laughing, excited. Sanjay refuses to make eye contact with the girls as they fall at his feet and he embarrassedly blesses them. His discomfort could not be more apparent.

On the other hand, I cannot help but stare at the younger one's eyes: they are unfocused and drowsy. Her movements too seem slightly unsteady. It is almost as though the psychedelic nature of the mandap has pervaded her mind; she clearly isn't there. Then I notice how young she is: the baby-fat in her cheeks, her general gawkiness. She could not have been eighteen.

Sanjay hastily shepherds us away, and soon we have said our zindabads and are bumping along in Navin's auto. I ask Sanjay if he noticed anything at all about the younger bride. He says he has not: 'I feel very uncomfortable doing these things in the first place; so I wasn't paying attention.'

Had the poor girl been fed opium? Perhaps just enough to allow her to sleepwalk through the evening, numbing both the loss of leaving and the pain of spending the night in a strange man's arms?

Ironically, the women seemed to be most encouraging of the practice. That part was the hardest to swallow—not the kohl-lined, drowsy eyes of the young girl, but the excitement on everyone else's faces.

On our way back, we pass the baraatis who are still making their way to the hamlet. It is like any other baraat: the same humongous speakers blaring out auto-tuned voices; the crowd of sweaty men; the possessed gyrations; except, now, for the first time, these images are infused with a sense of foreboding and pathos, at least for me.

I look away, resisting the urge to beseech them to return to wherever they came from.

In 1914, Heera Dom wrote a poem in Bhojpuri titled 'An Untouchable's Lament'. Sincere and poignant, this piece of writing was a remarkable achievement, because Heera, as his surname indicates, was a Dom—an untouchable sub-caste that occupied the lowest rung of the caste hierarchy. In the early twentieth century, a Dom who could read and write was rare. Yet, here was Heera, who not only composed poetry but also managed to publish it in the premier Hindi magazine of its times, *Saravasti*. The first stanza of Heera's poem went:[49]

We are made to suffer day and night
Made to plead in front of the ruler
Even the Gods don't see our pain
How long will this suffering last?

So untouchable were his caste brethren, Heera writes, that even the Gods did not dare touch their lives:

Saved Prahlad by tearing a pillar
Saved Gajaraj from the clutches of Graha
When Duryodhana's brother played with dignity
You appeared and added a layer of clothing
Killed Ravana and seated Vibhishana
Lifted a mountain on your little finger
Why are you sleeping, not listening now
Are you afraid to touch us untouchables?

Traditionally, the chief occupation of the Doms in caste Hindu society is to burn corpses, releasing souls from their mortal remains. This, therefore, is the deep irony: despite being the 'gatekeepers of the heavens', the Doms are touched neither by caste Hindus nor, as Heera suggests, the Gods.

Have things changed in these intervening years? Thirty years after *An Untouchable's Lament* appeared in the *Sarasvati*, the scholar Ethel Merston, residing in a village about 180 kilometres west of Bhojpur, described the lone Dom man in her village thus:[50]

---

49 All translations are by the poet Abhishek Anicca, who did them at my request.

50 Merston, E., *Village Life by the Ganges*, Diocesan Press, Madras, 1950, p. 55.

> Our one and only dom is a very decent fellow who lives amongst the khattiks. This is rather rare, I'm told, for usually no caste man will allow a dom to live near him. But ours is a silent man, keeps himself to himself, has a decent wife, and everyone likes them, though he seems to have no special friends and takes no part in village matters. After an initial battle with him over the filthy way he kept the Burning Ghat, leaving dirty rags lying around from the bodies and not troubling to throw uncremated bodies into the deep current, midstream, so that they came to anchor on the sandbanks just opposite to the village, he became a model of all a dom should be.

A model Dom in the mid-1940s, therefore, was not worth mentioning by name, was rarely granted the privilege of living among caste Hindus, was untouchable and took no part in village matters. Except, of course, for painstakingly disposing of the dead.

Merston's book, *Village Life by the Ganges*, spanned the period 1939–46. In 1947, India became an independent country. The newly adopted Constitution was a radical document, introducing a series of provisions for Dalit upliftment: untouchability was abolished under Article 17;[51] equality was guaranteed under Article 14; Article 15 explicitly forbade discrimination on grounds of religion, race, caste, sex or place of birth;[52] and finally, Article 15(4) created space for affirmative

---

[51] Article 17 of the Constitution of India states, '"Untouchability" is abolished and its practice in any form is forbidden. The enforcement of any disability arising out of "Untouchability" shall be an offence punishable in accordance with law.'

[52] Article 15(1) states: The State shall not discriminate against any citizen on grounds only of religion, race, caste, sex, place of birth or any of them.
Article 15(2) states: No citizen shall, on grounds only of religion, race, caste, sex, place of birth or any of them, be subject to any disability, liability, restriction or condition with regard to—

action policies—such as caste-based quotas—for Dalits and backward castes.[53]

Like a sinking ant in a flowing gutter that's been thrown a leaf, these moves left Dalits afloat, but precariously so. As one Bihari Dalit poet—who chose to remain anonymous—evocatively wrote in the turmoil-driven 1960s, even an education or a degree did not guarantee escape from poverty:[54]

The university gave me
A bundle of paper,
Weighed down by that burden
I knocked at every door,
And today after having sold myself
For a whole month,
And emerged from the office,
I realize–
That there are a few coins in, my palm
But no rations in the bazaar ... Mother.
What kind of jungle have you brought me into?

It was not until 2015 that a Dom character featured as the lead in a mainstream Hindi movie. That movie was called *Masaan*. 'Masaan' is a colloquial version of the term 'smashaan',

---

(a) access to shops, public restaurants, hotels and places of public entertainment; or

(b) the use of wells, tanks, bathing ghats, roads and places of public resort maintained wholly or partly out of State funds or dedicated to the use of the general public.

53 Article 15(4) states: Nothing in this article or in clause (2) of article 29 shall prevent the State from making any special provision for the advancement of any socially and educationally backward classes of citizens or for the Scheduled Castes and the Scheduled Tribes.

54 This poem appeared in an article in the *New York Times* on 26 April 1974: https://www.nytimes.com/1974/08/26/archives/downtrodden-of-india-burst-angrily-into-literature-education-and.html.

or crematorium. A masaan is, of course, a Dom's traditional workplace.

In the film, Deepak Kumar is a sensitive Dom youth who embodies the contradictions of urban Dalits: his family continues to practice the traditional occupation of burning bodies, but he simultaneously pursues a degree in civil engineering. When he falls in love, he is both elated and afraid, for his love interest is a Tripathi, a high-caste Brahmin. She dies in a bus accident and he is devastated, but his intimate acquaintance with death, bestowed upon him by the rules of caste society, allows him to come to terms with it. In the movie, unlike the unemployed poet from the '60s, Deepak's degree translates into a job as a civil engineer in Allahabad.

The Deepak Kumar narrative arc would have been unthinkable in Heera Dom's or Ethel Merston's times. The luxury of a college education, the relative anonymity of an urban existence, the freedom to converse with—and fall for—Brahmin women, a respectable job in another city: each of these would have been considered a miracle in itself, together they would have represented an impossibility.

Deepak Kumar is, in the end, a creation of the fertile minds of writer Varun Grover and director Neeraj Ghaywan. Walking around rural Bihar (as opposed to the urban Varanasi that Deepak calls home), how likely are we to come across someone like him?[55]

---

[55] It would not be entirely unreasonable to expect Dom youth, even in urban settings, to continue to practice the traditional occupation. In the six-minute short piece *Dom Raja—The Untouchable Gatekeeper of Heaven*, the pre-teen son of Jagdeesh Choudhry, a Dom man in charge of cremating bodies

It turns out, not very likely at all.

To establish this, we turn to the Socioeconomic Caste Census,[56] one that painstakingly—and heroically—collected data from every household in India. The purpose of the census, conducted in the early 2010s, was to identify poor households, so that the government could target poverty-alleviation programmes. Data on a series of proxy indicators for household wealth were gathered. This allows the government, and researchers like myself, to rank households by wealth, creating what is called a 'wealth distribution'.

A person with the last name Dom occupies the bottom decile of this wealth distribution.

What does this mean?

In practical terms, *this*. Imagine you went to a Dom household in rural Bihar and showed them a checklist comprising the following items: whether they own *any* land, a fridge, a motorised vehicle, mechanical agricultural equipment or irrigation equipment; whether their living room has a concrete roof or a concrete wall; whether the house has three or more rooms, if someone pays income tax, or has a government job.

Now, having shown someone from the Dom household this list, ask them to strike off the indicators that apply to their household. The typical Dom household will return the checklist as it was handed to them.[57]

Indulge me a little more in this thought exercise: you, the survey enumerator with a checklist in hand, walk out of the

---

by the Ganga in Varanasi, declares: 'When I grow up, I will work on the ghats and help my father, work and rule my kingdom [the cremation business]!'

[56] The official website is available here: https://secc.gov.in/.

[57] All data is based on my own calculations using the SECC rural data for Bihar. For the technically inclined, the median number of indicators checked off is 0, the mean is 0.57.

Dom household. Your next household on the list is headed by a Mr Manjhi, who lives in the neighbouring hamlet.

In the sweltering heat, you walk past the three houses in the Dom colony that lie at the western edge of the village, separate from everyone else's. You walk past the mud houses with their thatched roofs; the brown-grey damp earth by their low doors; the old, cataract-eyed woman flashing you a toothless smile; the party of three dark-skinned, unclothed children, the youngest with a premature paunch, who are too busy playing with straws of hay to throw you a second look; the white plastic bucket and its metal, rusted counterpart; the open drain that a solitary pig lords over.

A narrow path between two barren plots of land leads you to the Manjhi tola, which, while closer to the centre of the village than the Dom cluster, is still separated from the heart of the village by a path that circumvents a large, near-dry NREGA-constructed open pond.

At the entrance to the Manjhi tola, you are greeted by more raucous children with muddy hair, shooting stones at a yelping stray; there are more mud hovels, tightly packed together; more thatched roofs, more dark entrances, more dung on the walls, more sarees hung on clotheslines, appearing all the more bright against the pale greys and browns of everything else; a solitary bhains is nonchalantly chewing its cud and snorting away to glory.

A few questions to passers-by for directions, their roundabout responses and random walks in the afternoon sun, and you find yourself standing by Mr Manjhi's hut.

Luckily, he is home and willing to speak with you.

He asks if you want water. You gratefully accept, wiping the sweat off your brow with a drenched handkerchief. He is momentarily taken aback, but quickly smiles and rushes into the darkness of his home, and returns with a steel lota and a tumbler. He fills the glass with water and nonchalantly tosses it away: the glass is clean. He then fills it again and offers it to you. You gulp down the water.

You then get down to business. You hand him the checklist and ask him to strike off the items that apply to him.

Mr Manjhi cannot read,[58] so he asks you to read them off: '*Hum haan bolenge.*' (I will say yes whenever you read an indicator that applies to me.) You oblige.

He never says 'haan'.

From thought experiments to hard, cold numbers: data from the past decade indicates that a Dalit in Bihar was likelier to die at birth than his or her non-Dalit counterparts.[59] If they survived childbirth, they had lower birthweights, attained fewer years of schooling, had lower lifetime incomes, fell ill more, were raped more, were–barring a few exceptions–almost invisible in the public sphere and died much younger than everyone else.

---

[58] This illiteracy, when compounded with other socioeconomic realities, has stark consequences. This is best epitomised in this Musahar folk song:

Ek sau rupaiyaa karja delko
Hajar par leke nisaan
Anpadh jaan ke sab loot lelko
Mangani mein gelo jaan
(A hundred rupees' loan he gave
After making the paper for a thousand
Because illiterate I was, he robbed all I had
In vain, the life was wasted)

See: Kumar, Arun, 'Culture, Development and the Cultural Capital of Farce', *Economic and Political Weekly*, Vol. 41, No. 40, 2006, pp. 4281-4285+4271-4291.

[59] Sanjukta Chaudhuri, 'Excess Female Infant Mortality and the Gender Gap In Infant Care In Bihar, India', *Feminist Economics*, 21:2, 2015, pp. 131–161, DOI: 10.1080/13545701.2014.999007.

And yet, there is resentment in our cities and villages when government jobs or educational opportunities or political positions are reserved for Dalits.

In May 1987, the then Bihar chief minister, Bindeshwari Dubey, passed an ordinance mandating reservation for the post of mukhiya in the upcoming panchayat elections.[60] Dubey was a trade unionist leader and a Congress party member who had been handpicked by Prime Minister Rajiv Gandhi to lead Bihar. Two years into his term, Dubey was floundering, fighting in-party rivals in the state legislature, a hostile media and a collapsing state. Mired in clashes between Maoist low-caste peasant groups and upper-caste armies, or 'senas', of Rajputs and Bhumihars, Bihar saw rampant corruption and skyrocketing hunger: a state of turmoil that would continue to define it for years to come.

The case for reservation was almost too straightforward. Bihar had over one crore Dalits spread across its 11,387 panchayats. The deputy speaker of the Bihar State Assembly said that a mere six (six!) of those panchayats had a Dalit mukhiya.[61]

Dubey's rivals, both within and outside the party, were quick to criticise the move. They questioned the mechanism used to push through this legislation—an ordinance by the executive as

[60] Sections 2 and 3 of the Bihar Panchayat Raj (Amendment) Ordinance, 1987 amended Sections 10 and 11 of the Bihar Panchayat Raj Act, 1947 to reserve the seat of mukhiya in certain gram panchayats for members of the SC/ST communities, based on their percentage in the total population of a district.

[61] As cited in Farzand Ahmed, 'Bihar Government ordinance reserving post of 'mukhiya' for SC/ST takes many by surprise', *India Today*, https://www.indiatoday.in/magazine/indiascope/story/19870515-bihar-government-ordinance-reserving-post-of-mukhiya-for-scst-takes-many-by-surprise-798858-1987-05-15. This number, however, may be an underestimate.

opposed to a law by the legislature—and its timing, when caste tensions were rising to a feverish pitch and barely two months prior to the next panchayat elections.[62]

Within the fortnight, the ordinance had been challenged in the Patna High Court via writ petitions by six incumbent mukhiyas. The court deemed that elections could not be held till the matter was resolved. Thus, the panchayat elections of the summer of 1987 were postponed. By now, Bihar had not held elections at the panchayat level for nine years.

Bindeshwari Dubey's government fell in 1988. Rajiv Gandhi, the prime minister who hand-picked him, was assassinated in 1991. Dubey himself died in 1993 in Madras. And finally, in 2001, a full fourteen years after the ordinance was floated and challenged, Bihar held its panchayat elections.

But reservation still had to wait until the new chief minister, Nitish Kumar, passed the Bihar Panchayat Raj Act, 2006.

The story of how and why it took eighteen years from ordinance to law makes for a perfect potboiler, featuring, inter alia, upper-caste prejudice, ingenious reinterpretations of Gandhian village republics, courtroom tamashas, a volte-face by a colourful and contradictory backward-caste politician, a transformative legislation and a last-ditch, grand battle in the courts.

---

[62] Ideally, an ordinance should be promulgated only to address an emergency or deal with an urgent issue when the legislature is not in session. Since the promulgation of an ordinance does not involve scrutiny, discussion and voting by the legislature, it is deemed to be a subversion of the democratic process. Further, since this ordinance was impugned barely a few days after the state legislature had been in session, there were concerns regarding the executive's intentions and its abuse of power. More recently, in 2017, a seven-judge bench of the Supreme Court in *Krishna Kumar Singh v. State of Bihar*, made a series of pronouncements with respect to the executive's ordinance-making power, including that an ordinance can be subjected to judicial scrutiny and that it does not automatically create enduring effects.

Let's start in 1987, where it all began.

Kali Charan Singh Yadav, the pramukh of the Panchayat Samiti of Bodh Gaya, was Petitioner Number 1 in a writ filed against Dubey's potentially transformative–if audacious and opportunistic–1987 ordinance reserving posts for mukhiyas. Of the remaining five, all were mukhiyas and (at least) one was a Dalit, a certain Mr Janardan Paswan. This carried great symbolic value. Both probabilistically and practically, it was unlikely that the other petitioners were Dalits. After all, why would multiple Dalit petitioners oppose reservations in their favour? Yet, the case came to be known as *Janardan Paswan v. State of Bihar*.[63]

'The history of the Supreme Court's "reservations" jurisprudence,' the prolific constitutional scholar Gautam Bhatia notes, 'is the history of two competing visions of equality.'[64] In one view, the Constitution–and Article 14 (the right to equality) in particular–was viewed as largely 'caste-blind' and reservations were only awarded in exceptional circumstances.[65] The second view, following *The State of Kerala v. N.M. Thomas*, turned this conventional understanding on its head. In the judgement, the court saw caste hierarchies as impediments to equal access to the state's resources. Reservations were fundamental to furthering the Constitution's vision of equality.

---

63 1987 SCC Online Pat 160: AIR 1988 Pat 75 (FB): 1987 PLJR 875 (FB): (1987) 35 BLJR 853 (FB).

64 Gautam Bhatia, *The Transformative Constitution: A Radical Biography in Nine Acts*, HarperCollins, Noida, 2019, p. 75.

65 This view of the Supreme Court is reflected in *State of Madras v. Champakam Dorairajan*, 1951 SCR 525; *General Manager, Southern Railway v. Rangachari*, 1962 SCR (2) 586; *M.R. Balaji v. State of Mysore*, 1963 Supp. (1) SCR 439 and *T. Devadasan v. Union of India*, 1964 SCR (4) 680. The common thread running through all these cases was a certain aversion towards reservations. The court constructed individuals as devoid of their personal characteristics and class identity (such as caste, gender, religion),

In support of this view, the *N.M. Thomas* judgement relied on Article 15(4), which stated that 'Nothing ... shall prevent the State from making any special provisions for the advancement of any socially and educationally backward classes of citizens or for the Scheduled Castes [SCs] and the Scheduled Tribes [STs].' Articles 14, 15, and 16 were held to form 'part of a string of constitutionally guaranteed rights' that supplemented one another. Special provisions under Articles 15 and 16 for Dalits and backward classes were not to be read as exceptions to Article 14, but as the enforcement of equality guaranteed under Article 14.[66]

Appearing for the State of Bihar in *Janardan Paswan*, Advocate General Ram Balak Mahto argued that reservations for mukhiyas simply furthered this vision of the Constitution.

The court disagreed and held that while *N.M. Thomas* ruled in the case of reservations in government jobs and educational institutions, its applicability did not extend to electoral positions:

> When Article 15 (4) is read in the context of Article 29 (2), as it inevitably must be, it is more than plain that the purpose was in terms related to the *denial or grant of admission into educational institutions.* Neither the earlier three clauses of Article 15, nor Article 29 (2), to which reference is made in the very beginning of clause (4), has the least reference or connection with electoral or franchise rights. Nor would they have any relevance to political advancement through the *curious and dubious methodology of reservations* therein. (Emphasis mine)

---

thus adopting a caste-blind approach towards reservations. Furthermore, emphasising the 'exceptional' nature of reservations, the court capped it at 50 per cent. Gautam Bhatia notes that this was done to ensure that exceptions could not swallow up the rule of equality and non-discrimination.

[66] The historical and social inequality of backward classes was sought to be corrected through differential treatment, thereby fulfilling the vision of equality for all.

On five separate occasions, the *Janardan Paswan* judgement makes reference to the 'poison' of reservation, which, when applied to the electoral sphere, spreads 'divisiveness' among people. The court further noted that reservations for mukhiyas were the 'thin end of a wedge' and it could not 'but lead to deleterious State level and even National level ramifications'. By way of explanation, it added:

> [S]uch a poison may spread to other units of local self-government and a carte-blanche power would vest in the State to make reservations of the Chairman of the Municipal Committees or the Notified Area Committees and, for that matter, of the Mayors of the Corporation ...

In the court's eyes, reservation was a many-armed poisonous beast, its malignant tentacles encircling every last wing of government, spreading hatred and dividing society. We have been down this path before, the court reminded everyone in its judgement, during the time when the British introduced separate electorates for Muslims and Hindus and successfully 'divided and ruled':

> It was highlighted on behalf of the petitioners that disastrous results culminating from separate electorates and reservation of seats led first to a divisiveness of the polity and then to a division of the country may well come to be repeated at a lower plane. Perhaps, the fears expressed on behalf of the petitioners may be somewhat exaggerated but it cannot be said that they are wholly ill-founded.

In equating reservation for mukhiyas with separate electorates for Muslims under the British Raj, the court had indulged in three cavalier leaps of logic: first, it had conveniently conflated separate electorates with reservations. While, in both cases, only minority candidates contested elections, separate electorates allowed only minorities to vote, while reservations allowed everyone a vote. Thus, under reservations, even if non-minorities could not contest, they had a say in who would be their leader.[67]

Second, the court seemed to have forgotten that independent India, with a democratically elected government held in check by a liberal Constitution, was a very different country from the unfree India that functioned under rulers whose explicit intention was to divide the populace. In the hands of a state committed to the equality of its people, reservations were likely to be sweet nectar—not poison—to the Dalits.

Third, the court had ignored the fact that under Part XVI of the Constitution, reservations *had*, in fact, been introduced in political positions, namely state legislatures. This had caused no new schisms between communities, no fresh divisive poison had flowed.[68]

In exaggerating the fears of the 'poison of reservation', the court had channelled a version of Gandhi's own opposition

[67] The judgement also conflated the right to vote with the right to contest in an election. While the Constitution provides for universal adult suffrage under Articles 325 and 326, the right to contest an election is a statutory right, which is to be exercised in accordance with statutory provisions. In *Jumuna Prasad Mukhariya v. Lachhi Ram* (1955 SCR 608), the Supreme Court held that the right to stand as a candidate and contest an election is not a common law right but a statutory right. The Patna High Court, in *Janardan Paswan* (AIR 1988 Pat 75), did not take this pronouncement of the apex court into consideration while waxing eloquent on franchise rights. It held that equality of franchise will be affected if the candidature of a person, for whom the elector wishes to vote, is barred, thus erroneously conflating equal franchise rights with the right to contest an election.

[68] The advocate general had cited Part XVI of the Constitution in his defence of reservations. Part XVI explicitly permitted provision for reservation of seats in favour of Scheduled Castes and Scheduled Tribes in state legislatures. Perhaps it was not too much of a stretch to extend this to local government bodies? The court disagreed and held that the provisions made in Part XVI were meant to be 'exceptions', their mandates limited only to the Lower Houses of State Legislatures. They were also 'ephemeral', originally envisaged to cease in ten years.

to separate electorates for Dalits. In the 1930s, Gandhi was worried that separate electorates (again, *not* reservations) for the 'depressed classes', the term then used to describe Dalits, would divide Hindu society. He famously fasted to force Ambedkar's hand in the Poona Pact (a fact that caused much bitterness in the latter). Six decades hence, the Patna High Court had taken Gandhi's concerns–which were of a somewhat controversial, if not spurious, nature–and had imagined a far more potent version of them in a much more benign social atmosphere.

Remarkably though, this was *not* the most egregious reading of Gandhi the court had endorsed in the judgement.

For this, we must briefly turn to the notion of 'single posts' and the jurisprudence surrounding it. Over the decades, high courts and the Supreme Court have ruled that if there is only a single position available–say, for instance, one academic job in a department–it could not be reserved since this would violate the principle of equality that Article 14 espoused.[69] Furthermore, and more practically, if reservation was to be extended to, say, 16 per cent of positions, what exactly did it mean to reserve 0.16 seats out of one?

How did this 'solitary position' jurisprudence apply to the question of reservation for the post of mukhiya in Bihar–of whom, in 1987, there were a total of 11,387? Once more channelling the Mahatma, the court most mischievously (a term the court used twice to describe the ordinance) sided with the petitioners' arguments. This was a farce in three parts: *reproduce*, *reinterpret*, *reject*.

[69] Unless the Constitution provides otherwise, as seen in Article 243D, this law continues to hold good. As recently as 2019, in *R.R. Inamdar v. State of Karnataka* (2019 SCC OnLine SC 1603), the Supreme Court reiterated that there can be no reservation of a solitary post.

Part 1: Reproduce

The court cited chapter 24 of Gandhi's *India of My Dreams*, where under the heading 'Every village a republic', the Mahatma wrote:

> My idea of village Swaraj is that [the village] is a complete republic, independent of its neighbours for its own vital wants ... Independence must begin at the bottom. Thus every village will be a Republic or Panchayat having full powers. It follows, therefore, that every village has to be self-sustained and capable of managing its affairs even to the extent of defending itself against the whole world ...

We have, in previous chapters, encountered Gandhi's idealised dream of village republics. This was a vision, as I have argued earlier, that was relegated to the Directive Principles, and went almost wholly unrealised because of Ambedkar's scepticism and the centralising tendencies of the Nehruvian state.[70]

And yet, here was the Patna High Court excavating the Mahatma's buried dreams from under four decades of lived history that had run a course entirely contrary to his words.[71]

Part 2: Reinterpret

K.P. Verma, appearing for the petitioners, used this anachronistic reproduction of Gandhi to point out that, logically speaking, 'the post of Mukhiya is an office and if the village is a unit by itself, the same is the solitary post of its executive head'. In plain English, he made the patently absurd claim that the 11,387 villages of Bihar were, in fact, *independent republics*. Rural Bihar,

[70] Until 1992, at least, when the Seventy-second Amendment was passed.

[71] In doing so, the Court deemed it more important to give effect to its interpretation of the ideals laid down in Article 40 of the Constitution than protect the fundamental rights guaranteed under Article 15. Article 40 is

in his contention, was not one state–a continuous whole–but a conglomeration of loosely connected villages.

Since both Gandhi and the DPSP seemed to agree with this view, it made sense to see each village as an independent unit in itself and each mukhiya as a solitary position, a world unto himself or herself.

How then can one reserve a proportion of one?

Part 3: Reject

The court did not merely endorse Verma's arguments, but went on to state that his opposite number, the advocate general, was 'on his weakest wicket' while rebutting the 'solitary position' claim. Perhaps Ram Balak Mahto was simply too busy picking his jaw up from the floor. In any case, after citing Gandhi and concurring with–and expounding upon–Verma's imaginative take on the Mahatma's views, the court ruled that:

> [E]ven assuming entirely for the sake of argument that Article 15(1) is applicable (without in the least holding so), nevertheless the reservation of the solitary post of Mukhiya in the self-contained unit of a Panchayat exclusively for scheduled castes and scheduled tribes is patently excessive, unreasonable and violative of the rule of equality.

---

under Part IV of the Constitution, where all Directive Principles of State Policy (DPSPs) are enshrined while Articles 14 and 15 are under Part III, where all the fundamental rights are guaranteed. DPSPs were formulated as guidelines/ideals that the state should strive towards fulfilling and are generally regarded as non-justiciable unless the court brings forth a DPSP within the ambit of a fundamental right. For example, the Supreme Court has read Article 39A (DPSP providing for free legal aid) along with Article 21 (right to life) to hold that free legal aid is a fundamental right. However, fundamental rights are always enforceable. While DPSPs and fundamental rights are to be read harmoniously as far as possible, in case of any conflict, fundamental rights always override DPSPs.

The Patna High Court's excesses went well beyond this creative reading of Gandhi. It conveniently narrowed down the holding in N.M. *Thomas*, and its own application of it in an earlier case relating to reservation for backward classes, where it had recognised that the provision for co-option of a member from the backward classes was made to ensure the representation of these castes and classes in local bodies.[72] In its narrowed-down reading, the court failed to acknowledge that political participation is necessary for social and educational advancement. Further, while the court did acknowledge that Articles 14 and 15 were facets of the same coin, it did not delve into a deeper analysis.[73] And thus, Bindeshwari Dubey's 1987 ordinance failed to pass muster at the high court. In a reflection of how important the matter was, the decision was delivered in 1987 itself.

By now, several other high courts had upheld Dalit reservation in panchayats.[74] Dalit mukhiyas were common in states like Karnataka and Andhra Pradesh.

The Dalits of Bihar, however, had to wait.

---

72 *Ramakanat Choudhary v. State of Bihar*, 1979 SCC OnLine Pat. 75.

73 Neither did the court discuss the arbitrariness of the law at length or show how it was arbitrary, nor did it apply the older test of reasonable classification under equal protection law. It merely cited *E.P. Royappa v. State of Tamil Nadu*, 1974 (4) SCC 3 (the landmark case on arbitrariness under Article 14), and then referred to American jurisprudence on the equal right to vote, which was a different issue from reservation. It ignored that race-conscious preferential treatment had been upheld in the US as well.

74 The Andhra Pradesh High Court in *C. Satyanarayana Reddy v. State of AP*, 1987 SCC OnLine AP 286; the Allahabad High Court in *Jaswant Singh v. State of UP*, 1989 SCC OnLine All. 43, and the Karnataka High Court in *N.B. Hullara v. State of Karnataka*, 1988 ILR Kar. 2771 all upheld reservations

The Constitution (Seventy-third Amendment) Act, 1992—better known as the 'Seventy-third Amendment'—created the space for strong, formal panchayati raj institutions across the country. The amendment recognised that such institutions thus far had failed to 'acquire the status and dignity of viable and responsive people's bodies'.[75] In diagnosing the causes for these failures, it spoke of the 'insufficient representation of weaker sections like Scheduled Castes [and] Scheduled Tribes'.

This then cleared the path for reservation for panchayat heads across the country. The newly inserted Article 243(D) of the Indian Constitution now explicitly allowed for reservations for SCs, STs and women in panchayats.

Bihar soon followed suit and the incumbent Lalu Prasad Yadav government passed the Bihar Panchayat Raj Act in 1993. Pat came the writ petitions in its wake, challenging the Act. This time, the petitioners had a steeper hill to climb: the Seventy-third Amendment acted as a bulwark against challenges to reservations using the usual route. Articles 14 and 15 could no longer be invoked.

However, the ghost of *Janardan Paswan* continued to work its powerful sorcery. In *Krishna Kumar Mishra v. State of Bihar*, the Patna High Court ruled that, while Article 243(D) applied in all instances where there were multiple posts to reserve in a panchayat—say ward members, of whom there were (roughly) thirteen—it found no reason to differ with *Janardan Paswan* on the question of solitary posts, stating quite plainly that:

No reservation can be made against solitary seats like the mukhiya of a panchayat.

---

for Dalits or other backward classes in gram panchayats under Article 15(4) of the Constitution.

[75] For the text of the amendment, see here: https://www.mhrd.gov.in/sites/upload_files/mhrd/files/upload_document/73amend.pdf.

This was in 1996. It took a further five years before elections were held and a full decade before reservations were implemented.

Why so?

A casual reading of the intervening years would perhaps lay the blame at the feet of India's slothful judicial system. Indeed, the years between 1996 and 2001 were marked by much legal wrangling across the Patna High Court and the Supreme Court, with multiple petitions and counter-petitions being filed.

However, a more careful reading will throw up the role that the canny chief minister Lalu Yadav played in perpetuating inertia. Yadav, champion of the backwards and the downtrodden, was—as Sankarshan Thakur's glorious moniker 'subaltern saheb' indicates—full of contradictions. In his decade and more at the helm of state politics in Bihar, he brought about tremendous social churn, upending entrenched power hierarchies. With his fiery, sarcastic speeches and blasé antics, Lalu Yadav instilled pride in the hearts of the backward castes and the Dalits. His revolution was one not of violence, but nonchalance and insouciance, disregard and smugness. 'Look at me,' he seemed to say to his followers, 'I am one of *you*, and yet, I laugh at these hierarchies, and everyone laughs *with* me!'

But Yadav also served as more than a symbol. Behind the show and pomp lay a calculating method. He systematically went about dismantling the state bureaucracy, that hallowed bastion of the upper castes. Posts were purposely left vacant, funds unutilised, directions by personnel unheeded, their auras diminished. In doing so, he empowered his MLAs, mostly from powerful backward and lower castes, who were now free to govern as they pleased. The see-saw of power between politicians and bureaucrats—or, isomorphically, backward and elite castes—tilted decisively towards the former. As Jeffrey

Witsoe has pointed out, Lalu Yadav sacrificed *development* for *democracy*,[76] bringing the state and its elected legislators closer than ever to the poor. The state may have been in an emaciated condition, rendered hollow and leaking, but that was a price Yadav willingly paid.

This upender of hierarchies, harbinger of progressive social change, would have–*should* have–backed devolution of powers to panchayats and reservations for the marginalised. The unpredictable Yadav did nothing of the sort. His 1993 Act, in fact, contained stringent provisions to perpetuate state government control over panchayati raj institutions. When, in 1996, the Patna High Court partially struck down the 1993 Act in *Krishna Kumar* and the Supreme Court consequently dismissed all mukhiyas and ordered administrators to take over, Yadav was in no hurry to sort things out. He simply waited and watched as the years rolled by.

One could speculate on the reasons for his reluctance to speed things up. Lalu Yadav's instincts were to take power out of the hands of the elite upper castes and concentrate them in the hands of his MLAs and, through them, himself. He had an inherent distrust of organised structures like panchayati raj institutions, which he saw merely as comprising another 'bunch of self-seekers, middle men'.[77] His carefully crafted image of a commoner chief minister–a subaltern saheb–necessitated that there be only a bare minimum level of visible layers between him and his people. Also, over the past decade, Yadav's core base comprised of a carefully crafted coalition of powerful backward

---

[76] Jeffrey Witsoe, *Democracy against Development: Lower-Caste Politics and Political Modernity in Postcolonial India*, University of Chicago Press, Chicago, 2013.

[77] G. Kumar, 'Panchayat Elections: Overcoming State's Resistance', *Economic and Political Weekly*, 2001, 36(29), p. 1683.

castes and Muslims, which had arranged itself staunchly behind him. He worried that the introduction of elections would create friction, and the two groups would clash in a substantial number of panchayats.[78]

In 2000, the Patna High Court, growing impatient with Yadav's dithering ways, ordered the government to hold panchayat elections.[79] Once more, in an attempt to keep the status quo going, he turned to the Supreme Court for relief. To his dismay, the apex court broadly agreed with the high court.[80] The question of reservations, however, was still moot. The Supreme Court ruled that reservations be implemented for some posts, but not for mukhiyas. It was all so confusing that the State Election Commission had to seek a clarification from the Supreme Court. In the end, in April 2001, elections were held with no reservations for the post of the mukhiya.

The 2001 cohort of mukhiyas was a lopsided one, unrepresentative of its constituents. A mere 1.06 per cent of the 2001 cohort of mukhiyas were Dalits. Nearly three-fourths of Dalit mukhiyas were Paswans.

---

[78] Shaibal Gupta also makes the point that Lalu Yadav was too preoccupied with other political machinations to truly care about or understand the potential of panchayati raj institutions: 'Coming from the "cockney" segment of the local elite, Lalu Prasad could also never understand that decentralisation could develop provincial markets and trigger development. He was politically more engaged with the implications of the collapse of the upper caste citadel in the 1990 assembly elections. The subsequent elections of 1995 and 2000 further strengthened his social group, specially its upper segment. This put the question of "development" and the political purpose of decentralisation, like the land reform, on the backburner.' See: S. Gupta, 'New Panchayats and Subaltern Resurgence', *Economic and Political Weekly*, 2001, 36(29), pp. 2742–2744.

[79] *Nand Kishore Singh v Union of India*, 2000 SCC OnLine Pat. 412 (Patna High Court).

[80] A mention of this Supreme Court order is made in *Nand Kishore Singh v Union of India*, 2000 SCC OnLine Pat. 915 (Patna High Court).

This then was the sorry legacy of *Janardan Paswan*: a paltry sixty Paswan mukhiyas and about fifteen other Dalit mukhiyas, spread across Bihar's 7,120 panchayats.

A vastly underrated aspect of Nitish Kumar's personality is his voice. It has a deep, sonorous quality, at once commanding and sympathetic. The first time I heard him in person, in a large but sparsely filled conference room, it was as though he had surround-sound speakers for vocal chords. His voice possesses a characteristic that (in recent years especially) the man seems to lack somewhat: charisma. In the media's lazy denouncements of his inability to craft an aura, the alluring effect of his voice is forgotten.

In the telling of Bihar's turnaround since the Lalu years, scholars and commentators tend to focus on Nitish Kumar's role as Sushasan Babu–the man who brought good governance to the state.[81] If it has more than a semblance to a modern state and some law and order, Bihar certainly has Nitish Kumar to thank for the change.

Yet, here is another, underrated aspect of the man with the booming voice: he also *gave* voice to the marginalised. Nitish Kumar built on Lalu Yadav's chaotic social restructuring–filled with grand gestures of great symbolic significance–in a systematic, structured manner. He empowered the marginalised through legislation and targeted government action. Within a year of assuming the post of chief minister, his government

[81] Both Lalu Yadav and Nitish Kumar, alongside a battery of leaders who have influenced Bihar's political trajectory in the past many decades, participated in the Bihar Movement, led by the socialist Jayaprakash Narayan.

introduced and passed the Bihar Panchayat Raj Act, 2006.[82] The Act introduced roughly 1 per cent reservation for STs, nearly 17 per cent reservation for SCs, up to 20 per cent reservation for Extremely Backward Classes[83] and nearly 50 per cent reservation for women across all posts in panchayati raj institutions, including that of the mukhiya.

By 2006, in accordance with Article 243(D) of the Seventy-third Amendment, nearly every other Indian state had introduced reservations in favour of SCs, STs and women for the post of mukhiya. Bihar was late to the party, but was determined to make up for it. It did so by reserving more seats—50 per cent reservations for women and up to 20 per cent reservations for EBCs—and for longer tenures, ten years, as opposed to the conventional five years.

There was, however, one final hurdle to cross. Over 100 writ petitions invariably challenged the 2006 Act. Once more, the Patna High Court was called upon to pronounce its verdict. A three-judge bench in *Vijay Kumar Singh v. State of Bihar*[84] upheld the Act, finally exorcising the ghost of *Janardan Paswan*, stating:

> The pronouncement of this Court in Janardhan Paswan is no longer a good law, for subsequent to the said Judgment, Chapter-IX containing Article 243D was inserted in the Constitution and Krishna Kumar Mishra is an incorrect pronouncement of law, for the same was rendered without taking note of the mandate as well as the enabling provision

---

[82] Here, too, an ordinance—The Panchayat Raj Ordinance—preceded the Act.

[83] B.P. Mandal, the man who headed the Mandal Commission, the findings of which greatly furthered the OBC-reservation cause, hailed from Madhepura in Bihar.

[84] (2006) 2 PLJR 606 (FB).

contained in Article 243D of the Constitution, which was inserted after the pronouncement in Janardhan Paswan.

And thus, the high court brought down the curtains on a long-drawn-out saga of its own making.

Did reservation improve the lives of the Dalits of Bihar?

With Chinmaya Kumar—a dear friend and long-term collaborator, who spent his formative years in a village called Sutihara nestled against the Nepal border—I studied this question from the point of view of an empirical development economist. We focused mainly on the first cohort of Dalit mukhiyas who assumed power in 2006. Using an econometric technique called a 'regression discontinuity design', we compared two identical groups of villages, with the only difference being that some had a Dalit mukhiya and others did not. This technique allows us to make *causal claims*: statements that directly measure the consequences of the reservation policy.

As expected, the incoming cohort of mukhiyas who were Dalit looked different: they were much younger, had less wealth and were more likely to be illiterate than their non-Dalit counterparts.

We then measured their performance, using data on public goods—roads, schools, ration shops—from over 45,000 villages and private wealth data from 1.7 crore households of rural Bihar.

Here are the five key results we documented.

First, reservation did not affect village-level outcomes. In other words, despite Dalit mukhiyas being from obviously more disadvantaged backgrounds, they performed no worse than their non-Dalit counterparts. The average person in a Dalit-mukhiya-led village in 2011 enjoyed no fewer—or no more—public goods or private assets than in unreserved villages.

Second, reservation lowered inequality between Dalits and non-Dalits in villages: by 2011, thanks to reservation, more roads and schools were built in hamlets where Dalits resided. These were hamlets which had long been ignored. Also, the gap in household wealth between Dalits and non-Dalits reduced. Reservation, therefore, did not change the size of the pie, it changed *how* the pie was being distributed—with a larger share going to Dalits.

Third, these effects persisted even *thirteen years later*: when, in 2019, we sent teams back to these villages to survey thousands of households, we found that Dalits in villages reserved between 2006 and 2016 continued to be wealthier and had better access to public goods than their counterparts in unreserved villages.

Fourth, reservation increased the political participation of Dalits in local elections. In 2016, after ten years of reservation in villages, more candidates from Dalit backgrounds contested and won mukhiya and ward elections.

At this point, one may begin to wonder if the protests against reservations were misplaced. After all, while Dalits benefit, the average person in the village did no worse.

This brings us to our fifth and final result: some people did lose out because of reservation. These were individuals belonging to the traditional dominant elite sub-caste in the village (invariably non-Dalit sub-castes). This sub-caste would have most likely cornered electoral power in the absence of reservations. Their private wealth actually reduces when villages are reserved. This contributes to the reduction in inequality between Dalits and non-Dalits.[85]

---

85 But, because Dalits benefit, the average wealth of a household in the village remains unchanged.

Reservation, like many policies, creates winners and losers. The losers suffer a direct loss of access to de jure power.[86] This then hampers their ability to accumulate private wealth and reduces their primary claim to public goods—which is what makes them oppose such policies in the first place.

It would, however, be naive to think that the loss of material wealth or electoral power is the *only* reason the elite castes oppose reservation tooth and nail. Reservations are opposed because they endeavour to thwart the natural order of Indian society which for millennia has remained a certain way: the likes of Heera Dom scraped the bottom, the Bhumihars and the Rajputs ruled from above. To the elites, reservation is frightening because it not only seeks to end their rein at the top, but also attempts to place on the same pedestal as themselves those from a polluting, inferior stock. The twin notions of superiority and pollution, two sides of the caste coin, form the basis of the deep-rooted opposition to such policies.

---

86 The difference between de jure (by law) and de facto (in reality) power can be vast. Take quotas for women, for instance. Anyone who has done fieldwork in the villages of India will encounter the woman leader whose husband (mukhiya-pati) or father does their work. The woman is often reduced to signing papers. In Bihar, I have met Dalit mukhiyas who are controlled almost entirely by the powerful elite castes of the village.

Despite this, many studies (including Esther Duflo & Raghabendra Chattopadhyay, 'Women As Policy Makers: Evidence from a Randomized Policy Experiment in India', *Econometrica*, Vol. 72, No. 5, September 2004, pp. 1409–1443) have shown that reservation in favour of women makes women's lives better. Similarly, as my own research indicates, reservation in favour of Dalits improves the lives of Dalits.

How does one square these two facts? There are two points to note here: first, that not every reserved seat has been 'captured' by elites; second, even when a Yadav 'remote-controls' a Dalit mukhiya, the latter may still be able to influence some decisions. Taken together, this indicates that, in the coming years, when women and Dalits are further socially empowered, reservation will work even better.

Cambridge, 2015

In the months following my arrival in America—my first time living abroad—Sanjay and I chat every now and then [on the now outdated calling app Viber]. Much of the conversation revolves around him filling me in on the latest news from Muzaffarpur: the state had yet again run out of NREGA funds; a new group of saathis had joined the sangathan; a dharna was being planned, another dharna was successful; Jean Drèze had come visiting and had cycled to distant villages; Jeffrey Witsoe, Bihar's foremost anthropologist of the Lalu-Nitish years, had decided to live in Mahant Maniyari; one more journalist had come calling; someone's mother was ill, another had had a child; Sanjay's own children were moving homes and schools, from Delhi to Ratnauli to Ranchi; he was, once again, out of money.

On one occasion, he tells me that SPSS had been betrayed.

I ask him for details.

He explains that some SPSS saathis had colluded with the mukhiya of a village and had siphoned off some NREGA funds. Up until recently, the village's SPSS mazdoors had been protesting and fighting against the mukhiya's corrupt ways. The mazdoors were mostly Dalit women and had had considerable success, having managed to demand—and organise—multiple NREGA projects in their village. The mukhiya, much like his counterparts in Ratnauli and Mahant Maniyari, was sidelined. And the mazdoors, drawing strength from their numbers, had overcome the disadvantages of caste, class and gender.

The mukhiya tried to threaten the mazdoors. When he realised it would not work, he cut a deal. He offered this group of mazdoors some money and asked them to sign on fake documents.

They did.

As he tells me this, Sanjay's voice, always bordering on the morose, is distraught.

I ask him to name the hamlet. He does. I wonder why the name sounds familiar.

'Have I been there?' I ask him.

'Of course,' he says, 'we went there for a wedding!'

5

Of the People, for the People

In 2011, as Sanjay Sahni first went about tallying official NREGA records with people's testimonies, he would often stop and attract a crowd around Salais Sthan in the panchayat of Mahant Maniyari. Salais Sthan–later christened NaREGA Chowk–is a brief respite in the chaos that is the Paswan tola, a tiny island of common land surrounded by a crowd of thatched dwellings. Its sanctuary-like aura comes from the sprawling banyan tree that lords over the chowk, with the idols of Lord Salais (Shailesh or Shiva) and Goddess Parvati at its feet.

A few years after Sanjay used Salais Sthan as a platform to springboard his movement, I remember sitting there, listening to the ageing Pavittar Paswan holding forth on the myth of Lord Shailesh. Paswan's eyes may have been clouded over by cataract, but he saw his characters almost too clearly, telling us the tale in such mind-numbing detail that all I recollect from that evening are silhouettes (of homes, trees and people) in the beige-grey evening light and the smell of fresh dung.

I cannot remember if the hero of this chapter, Mandesar Ram, was one of the silhouettes that day. If he was, it would have been apt. Mandesar is a man who keeps to the shadows—by which I do not intend to suggest that he is seedy or even a vigilante. He is simply a private man in a very public profession, never disappointed to be one among many. When you get to know him, you realise his passion for his work—unlike Sanjay's—does not manifest in showmanship but in indefatigability.

Mandesar Ram first spotted Sanjay Sahni at Salais Sthan in those early days. Sanjay then was a nondescript young man who lived in Delhi and was only just beginning to barge into people's imaginations. Bundles of papers in one hand, a loudspeaker in another and often with a videographer trailing him, he was, in people's eyes, one of many things: a charlatan, a saviour, a distraction, an irritant. On that day too, the crowd was clearly divided. Mandesar recalls: '*Kuchh log vishwas kar rahe the, kaafi log vishwas nahin kar rahe the.*' (Some believed him, many didn't.) Mandesar, however, listened to this ordinary-looking man speak and something in him wanted to give Sanjay a chance.

Up until that moment, Mandesar's own life had mirrored that of many others who lived and grew up in circumstances like his. He was born into a Dalit family of mazdoors, the only boy among his many siblings. His father, who crushed stone for a living, wanted better for his son and sent him to the local private school. On his days off from school, the young boy would accompany his father to work. The sight of his father toiling away under the harsh sun—veins popping on his sinewy arms—made him uneasy. Mandesar felt the best way he could help his family was by quitting school and working full-time.

So it came to be that the twelve-year-old Mandesar became a child migrant worker in India's gigantic informal sector—much like Sanjay Sahni, actually. By the time he was twenty, Mandesar had traversed the breadth of the country and was working at its western edge, in the town of Jamnagar. A former princely state, Jamnagar is home to (aside from a wealth of cricketing riches) the world's largest oil refinery.

It was in this very refinery that Mandesar worked as an escape holder.

'Escape holder?' I asked him, as we spoke over the phone, just to confirm. It felt like a perfectly believable even if unfamiliar, and yet oddly precise, name for a casual worker in a refinery.

He said: 'Haan, escape holder.'

I asked him to describe his job.

When a pipe burst in the giant oil storage tanks or elsewhere in the refinery, Mandesar and his team of three other mazdoors would quite literally swing into action. Hanging from a safety belt, they would go about constructing ladder-based platforms. A group of four would work on constructing the platform ground-up, each man to a pillar, building a rung of the ladder, then mounting it to build the next level, and so on until they reached the required height for the platform to be constructed. Engineers would then scale these platforms to fix the pipes.

Mandesar told me that he had built platforms as high as 110 metres.

That is nearly thrice as tall as India Gate.

'*Jhool ke kaam karte the. Kaafi dangerous tha; darr bhi lagta tha,*' he said matter-of-factly. (We would work suspended. It was very dangerous; I would be scared too.) On the phone, I could hear him almost chuckle. '*Lekin kya karein,*' he added, '*ghar–pariwaar chalana tha.*' (I had to run a home, support a family.)

I asked Ashwin Shetty, an old school friend, who worked as a site manager at a power plant in Jamnagar about the lives of these 'escape holders'. He speculated that 'escape holders' were a species endemic to refineries, having never come across one in all the power plants he had worked in. Where he had been, the type of work Ram described was usually performed by a group of workers called 'scaffolders'.

Only later, as I go over my notes from the call with Ashwin, do I make the connection: just like 'dayabharsan' is diversion and 'aidbhise' is advice (and, indeed, Mandesar is Mandeshwar), 'escape holders' is Bihari for 'scaffolders'.

Ashwin reckoned that, roughly speaking, two scaffolders die every year at these plants.[87] He had spent two years as a site manager and quit because of the risks involved. Once, inside the coal plant he was managing, he had climbed a low scaffolding—maybe 10–15 feet high—to test a pipe carrying hot coal, when an adjacent pipe burst and let out hot fumes. The workers who knew the plant like the back of their palms exited swiftly, while supervisors like Ashwin, who did not know the shortcuts out, barely escaped the fiery cauldron that the plant had become. Ashwin put in his papers soon after. 'It is risky,' he told me over the phone, 'I can see why the workers are scared.'

Mandesar Ram hung off scaffoldings in Jamnagar for ten years.

Tired of living on the edge and tired of being so far away from home, Mandesar returned to Muzaffarpur. He worked at the Narayanpur Anant Railway Station, as a loader in the goods trains. The pay was lower, but the life was safer.

A year into this new life, he first encountered Sanjay Sahni at Salais Sthan. Mandesar always wanted to do something for his people—as he put it, 'samaaj seva', or social work—and, in Sanjay, he found a kindred spirit. Over the next few years, he stuck close to Sanjay and watched, and sometimes contributed to, the events that played out: the Mathew-commissioned audit, the events that unfolded after the murder of the lawyer Ram Kumar Thakur, the birth of BMW and its sister SPSS, the rise

---

[87] *In A Free Man* (Random House, Delhi, 2012), Aman Sethi writes poignantly of Rehaan, a young worker who falls to his death at a construction site:

'Dropped off a tall ladder, these bones shatter, these muscles tear, these tendons snap, and when they do, they leave behind a crumpled shell in the place of a boy as beautiful and agile as Rehaan.'

of the mazdoors of Muzaffarpur, the dharnas and the gheraos, the victories and the betrayals, the unexpected kindness of a few in power and the more expected brutality of the state.

By 2015, Mandesar Ram had graduated to being a 'half-timer' with the sangathan. He kept diligent records of projects undertaken, accounted for funds spent and accompanied Sanjay to all his meetings with local members of government: the mukhiya, the BDO, the District Rural Development Authority (DRDA) director and the district magistrate. For his services, the sangathan paid him half the going rural minimum wage: a princely sum of Rs 80 per day. A further year on, in recognition of his indispensability, he was promoted to being a 'full-timer'.

My first clear memory of Mandesar is from some time in the summer of 2016. He was, as I recall, skinny, dark-skinned, with small, bright eyes and baby-fat in his cheeks. He had unkempt black hair, almost Harry Potteresque. Unlike the other mazdoors, who preferred half-sleeve vests and dhotis, he wore cheap full-sleeve shirts and pants. Watching him operate around the office, I began to see his value, as a sort of foil to Sanjay. While the latter went about his business—chiding, cajoling, arousing, arguing and empathising with the mazdoors—Mandesar sat in perfect peace, smiling beatifically, parting with words carefully.

As the evening sun hung listlessly over the fields by the MNREGA Watch office, I remember Sanjay telling me: '*Mandesar Ram ward member hai.* [Mandesar is a ward member.] These women—' He paused to wave in the direction of Mandesri Devi and others who were chatting among themselves. '—they got him to contest and win. They distributed pumpflets [pamphlets] and did the door-to-door campings [campaigning] themselves! *Bas do din main sab kuchh kar liye.* [It was all done in two days.]'

An image formed in my mind: the searing April heat; the harvest season's frenzy giving way to a throbbing stillness; and in this melting summer, the middle-aged women of the sangathan visiting house after house, singing songs, distributing pamphlets and shouting slogans in support of their yuva ummeedwaar, young candidate, Mandesar.

He won the election by a margin of eleven votes.

Thus it came to be that Mandesar Ram, this invisible migrant child worker, this swinging scaffolder of Jamnagar, this loader of goods trains in Narayanpur Anant, this full-timer at Mahant Maniyari's Samaj Parivartan Shakti Sangathan, came to adopt a new avatar:

Ward Member, Ward No. 7, Ratnauli Panchayat.

What does it mean to be a ward member?

Let's begin with some numbers: Bihar has thirty-eight districts, 534 blocks, a shade over 8,400 panchayats and a whopping 1,14,000 wards. Every ward has, by law, an elected representative, called a ward member. Thus, we have 1,14,000 ward members, among whom there are about 57,000 women, 25,000 Dalits and 20,000 EBCs.

Some more numbers: on average, a ward has 225 households and roughly 1,000 residents. In densely packed Bihar, this would often amount to as little as five criss-crossing lanes of houses. Wards are often caste homogenous: it is not unusual to see a blur of Paswan or Yadav houses making up an entire ward.

Here is Mandesar breaking down the numbers from his ward for me, like he is dictating an order to the local kirana store owner: '*Dhai-sau Ram, pandrah Yadav, chaar-paanch Lalaji, do-teen Sahni, chaar-paanch Sah.*' (Two hundred and fifty Ram households, fifteen Yadavs, four–five Lalajis, two–three Sahnis, four–five Sahs.)

Mandesar Ram, therefore, came from a somewhat larger-than-usual ward (300 households as opposed to the standard 225), but a typically caste homogenous one, predominantly made up of Rams. The Rams are Chamars, a prominent Scheduled Caste group.

In the absence of reservations, a Dalit mukhiya was almost an oxymoron. The numbers never work in favour of Dalits: on average, they are a numerical minority, forming a sixth of the population of a panchayat. On the other hand, the story with wards, which tend to be segregated by caste, is slightly different. Ram's ward was not reserved for Dalits. Yet, the sheer weight of the numbers—80 per cent Dalit households in the ward—had allowed for him to be elected.[88]

One final number, central to the understanding of local government in Bihar: there are, on average, fourteen ward members and one mukhiya in the average panchayat.

Are mukhiyas then fourteen times as powerful as the average ward member? In more immediate terms, is Sunaina Devi—wife of late Raj Kumar Sahni, mukhiya of Ratnauli and tormentor-in-chief of the mazdoors of Muzaffarpur—exponentially more powerful than Mandesar Ram?

I would think so. Though, for reasons I explain below, I would also argue that things are changing and the scales are ever-so-slowly tipping in favour of the ward members. When I ask him for his views on this, over the crackle of a telephone line, seven seas away, Mandesar Ram chuckles and agrees.

[88] Mandesar's main opponents in the elections were Matheswar Ram and Lal Babu Rai (a Yadav). A Yadav's caste superiority was no match for the numerical dominance of the Rams in the ward.

Thc numbers can get us only so far. A metaphor, now: for a long while, ward members were the Trishankus of village politics in Bihar. Like that mythical ancestor of Rama who was stuck between the earth and the heavens, ward members appeared suspended, occupying a point somewhere in the hazy continuum between citizens and politicians. On paper, they were members of local government, a fact that distinguished them from citizens. Yet, the actual powers of local government rested firmly in the corner of the mukhiyas.

This was even more true for Dalit ward members. In 2007, the eminent sociologist (and prolific chronicler of the lives of Bihar's marginalised citizens) Sachchidananda published a book on Dalit members of local government in the state.[89] In the 'Case Histories' section, he reproduces first-hand accounts of ward members, curiously reformulated in stilted third-person.

The first subject in this section is Tetari Devi, a female Dalit ward member from the southwestern district of Rohtas. Barely literate, Tetari is in Sachchidananda's esteem, 'an empowered lady'. She complains to the author that the mukhiya of her panchayat worked arbitrarily, rarely consulting her or anyone else. He did not share his power with ward members. He never told her about government schemes or Red Cards (what the government-issued BPL cards are locally called: these are invaluable in order to gain access to any targeted benefits for the poor). The mukhiya in Tetari's panchayat distributed Red Cards in her ward. In all, she is 'satisfied with her work as a Ward member but unhappy with the activities of Mukhiya ...'

How did Tetari think things could improve for her?

In one word: power.

---

[89] See Sachchidananda, *Empowerment of Dalits Through Panchayati Raj: The Bihar Experience*, Serial Publications, New Delhi, 2007.

She felt that 'power has not been given to ward members. This [is] why [the] Mukhiya acts in an arbitrary manner. Ward members should be given financial and other powers for development work ... development can *pick up if financial powers are given to ward members.*' (Emphasis mine.)

Meena Devi, a ward member residing in the picturesque district of Purnia, echoes Tetari's sentiments. Sachchidananda notes: 'She suggested that financial power should be shared by the Mukhiya with the ward members.'

The accounts from ward members that follow in his book are emphatic in their agreement. Suhas Baitha says 'the Mukhiya does what he wants to do for his own benefit'; Ashok Rajak claims that 'the Mukhiya does not share his power'; sixty-six-year-old Roopkali Devi says: 'No Mukhiya ... wants to share power with the other representatives in the Panchayati Raj system.'

Travelling around Bihar in 2012, I vaguely remember attending a ward sabha in a village in Arrah. A ward sabha, as the name indicates, is the ward equivalent of the gram sabha. It is a participatory forum for ward members and their constituents to engage in public discussion and plan future development projects. While the mukhiya presides over the gram sabha (as we saw in Chapter 2), the ward member presides over the ward sabha.

Sadly, I took no notes of the ward sabha in Arrah, and looking back today, nearly a decade hence, I only remember a scattered set of undramatic images: a small clearing amidst low green shrubs; a tarpaulin sheet laid out for the participants; a group of about twenty villagers (mostly men) sitting around a ward member, a man in a white kurta-pyjama; a notebook and a ball pen in the ward member's hands; a grey-black Nokia phone lazing on the tarpaulin; a man seated in front of me, who had a long nose and protruding jaw.

I also remember a discussion about what projects to work on in the coming year under the NREGA. The ward member had no powers—or funds—to implement these projects. His only job, in this instance, was to propose a list of potential projects to the mukhiya, who then was supposed to incorporate these projects into the 'shelf of works' for the year. Therein lay the rub. As we saw in Chapter 2, there is many a slip twixt cup and lip.

I shuttled between Patna (my workplace) and Delhi (where my wife and her parents lived) throughout the second half of my PhD (2016–19). On one such occasion, I happened to be on the same flight as Prashant Kishor, India's best-known political consultant. Kishor was seated in the first row of the business class section. He had two spacious seats all to himself. Yet, like the ward member in Arrah, he wore an austere white kurta-pyjama. By the time I met him, he was already a full-fledged politician, a member of the Janata Dal United (JD[U]) and part of Chief Minister Nitish Kumar's inner circle.[90]

Kishor and I spoke on the flight, and he asked me to see him in Delhi. And so, a month later, I found myself outside his office, a large bungalow in the heart of Lutyen's

[90] In January 2020, Prashant Kishor was expelled from the JD(U) for 'anti-party activities', i.e. criticising the chief minister's support for the Citizenship Amendment Act and the National Population Register. See: https://timesofindia.indiatimes.com/india/jdu-expels-prashant-kishor-pavan-varma-for-anti-party-activities/articleshow/73731985.cms.

Delhi. Sitting in the waiting room, I was surrounded by a phenomenon uncommon outside Bihar: the sing-song, insouciant manner in which words escaped people's mouths and floated in the air, giving the phrase 'speech bubbles' a whole new meaning.

Kishor had a commanding urgency about him. He spoke rapidly, in staccato bursts, like an Aaron Sorkin character on a Zoom call with intermittent connection.

Wasting no time on pleasantries, he got straight to the point: he had read my work thoroughly and had some questions. These questions, I was surprised to note, would not have been out of place at an economics seminar. I spoke to Kishor about my work on caste and a formal complaints' system that the Bihar chief minister had recently launched, called a grievance redressal system (more on this in Chapter 6).

When the discussion on my research was done, Kishor swiftly moved on to other, more important topics. 'When you are studying complaints and the grievance redressal system,' he told me, 'I hope you also focus on the schemes that are creating the maximum number of problems for all: the Nal-Jal and Nali-Gali yojanas.'

The 'Nali-Gali' yojana sought to build nalis and galis, drains and lanes, in every ward in Bihar. The 'Nal-Jal', or piped water, yojana promised to deliver piped water to every household. These two schemes were part of Nitish Kumar's Saat Nishchay (Seven Resolves), a bouquet of government programmes focusing on everything from electricity to women's empowerment. Together, these seven aims formed the core of Nitish Kumar's development agenda for his ongoing term as chief minister.

Kishor told me: 'The chief minister has staked his political future on these schemes. That is a brave move: these schemes create all sorts of problems in the short run, but will only reap benefits many years from now.'

'*Samaaj ke liye bahut kuchh karna chahte hain*' (I want to do a lot for the society), Mandesar Ram tells me over the phone and adds, '*Lekin kuchh log hain jo bahut* disturb *karte hain*' (But there are a few who disturb me a lot).

Two years after Kishor told me about the piped-water scheme, Mandesar tells me of the problems he faces delivering piped water to all the households in his ward.

He had a bank account opened for his ward, had received funds from the state's treasuries, and had paid a contractor to lay pipes and taps all over his ward. He then installed a pump that would help draw groundwater. A final element was to power the pump via electricity. This was proving to be a major hurdle. Ratnauli's electricity access has improved dramatically in the past decade. When I first went there in 2012, four hours of electricity was all one would get in the Sahni houses. The situation was so poor that the local kirana store owner invested in an inverter that he would loan out for charging cell-phones. By the time I went there in 2019, the situation had neatly inverted: four-hour power-cuts were the norm now.

Mandesar's problem is to do with electricity, but has nothing to do with the power-cuts (or lack thereof). His uniquely twenty-first-century problem went back over two millennia to the dawn of caste society. In a nutshell, the Bhumihar landlords neighbouring his ward refuse to let electric lines pass through to Mandesar's ward via their fallow, unused lands. '*Khet bilkul khaali hain*' (The lands are fallow), Mandesar reiterates, and it is perhaps the only time I hear a tinge of exasperation in his otherwise placid voice.

'Why would they do this?' I ask him (though I know enough about Bhumihars in Bihar to surmise the reasons).

Mandesar's answer spans generations. His grandfather and their grandfathers worked on the lands of the Bhumihars. 'My grandfather would stand up as soon as he saw them pass,' he says. His grandfather would not look those paymasters in the eye; he would cast aside his chappals if he was wearing them. His father, upon coming of age decided to–along with some siblings and cousins work elsewhere, a fact that caused considerable resentment among the Bhumihars. Yet, his father played by some rules: no wristwatches in front of the Bhumihar men. 'They did not like seeing us owning things,' Mandesar explains.

By the time it was Mandesar's turn to make his place in the world, things had changed further. The Rams of his hamlet no longer worked on the lands of the Bhumihars. They now walked proudly past their former masters, heads raised, footwear and wristwatches intact. Some, like Mandesar, were now members of the local government.

'They don't want to see us like this, to see us prosper,' he says. Consequently, the Bhumihars do everything within their powers to create trouble. Even if it means, as in this instance, inventing a whole new law of untouchability: 'electric wires that pass through our lands shall not touch the lands of the Dalits'.

Mandesar wrote to the subdivisional magistrate (SDM) about the obstinate Bhumihars. Twice, the SDM sent a mistry, a skilled foreman, to take a look. On both occasions, the mistry recommended constructing an electric pole at the edge of the Bhumihar lands and having wires pass through. On both occasions, these suggestions were rebuffed. On a third occasion, a pole was finally installed. But the Bhumihars did not allow wires to be connected to the pole.

All he has to show for his efforts—Mandesar tells me—are electric poles without wires and taps without running water.

There are few better metaphors than that for how far Dalits have come since Mandesar's grandfather's times and how much more ground they need to cover.

Folded into Mandesar's saga of generational injustices is a subtle and remarkable tale of decentralisation. Earlier in this chapter, we encountered Tetari Devi, a Dalit ward member—'an empowered lady' who complained of not having enough power. 'Development can pick up,' she had said, 'if financial powers are given to ward members.' Then, we encountered Mandesar Ram, who like Tetari was a Dalit and a ward member, but had been elected to government a decade later. In *his* role as implementer of the piped-water scheme, Mandesar had received funds from the state's treasuries to hire a contractor to lay pipes and taps. In other words, he, unlike Tetari, commanded *financial powers* to implement development projects.

How did this come about?

The answer lies in Circular No. 6278 of the Panchayati Raj Department, Government of Bihar, passed on 23 September 2016. It mandated that the implementation of two key schemes under the chief minister's Saat Nishchay Yojana would come under a Ward Development Committee headed by the ward member. As per the circular, funds for the (catchy, rhyming) Nal-Jal and Nali-Gali yojanas were to bypass the mukhiya entirely, travelling from the state's treasuries to the account held by the Ward Development Committee. The ward member, as head of this committee, would use the funds to run these projects. These were not ordinary schemes. After all, in Prashant Kishor's opinion, the chief minister had staked a chunk of his political future on the piped-water scheme.

If history—and this book—teaches one anything about the mukhiyas of Bihar, it is *this*: their tolerance for the mildest threat to their autonomy is low. The two schemes, while important politically, constituted only a fraction of the total amount of money at the disposal of the mukhiyas, who controlled funds for everything from the Finance Commission's allocations to the NREGA.

That did not stop them from taking the battle to the courts.

In this instance, writ petitions were filed by 'Mukhiya Sanghs'[91] from across the state of Bihar—Saran, Patna, Paschim Champaran, Arwal—challenging the validity of Circular 6278. Once more, the petitioners sought refuge in the Constitution. They made three broad points: first, under Article 243G, panchayats were the main functional units of village self-government, not wards. So, all development works had to go through the panchayat and not directly to the wards; second, given that panchayats were paramount under the Seventy-third Amendment, it was not the prerogative of the state to tell panchayats *how* to implement schemes; third, there was no need to create a new Ward Development Committee when the Constitution and the Bihar Panchayat Raj Act, 2006 had already allowed for the creation of Public Works Committees and Standing Committees (these were, of course, headed by the mukhiya) that could easily do the same job.[92]

The high court agreed with the petitioners and asked the state to reconsider its grand devolution plans. Circular No. 6278 died a quiet death, replaced by another one issued a few

---

[91] Literally, 'Mukhiya Groups'.

[92] The court order can be found here: *Paschim Champaran Mukhiya Sangh v. The State of Bihar*, 17 May 2017, https://indiankanoon.org/doc/151117772/.

months later. In the circular, the state proposed a compromise: the schemes would still be implemented by the ward members, but the funds would be routed through the mukhiya.

This was allowed to pass.

Thus, under the new rules, Mandesar Ram was asked to set up a committee, though with a minor semantic twist. It would not be called the Ward Development Committee, but the Ward Implementation and Management Committee. The word 'development', for some reason, was deemed antithetical to the autonomy of the mukhiyas and the spirit of the Seventy-third Amendment.

This Ward Implementation and Management Committee would have a bank account of its own. Mandesar was free to hire contractors and implement projects. However, the funds no longer bypassed Mandesar's mukhiya, Sunaina Devi, but flowed *through* her. She would first access the state's pool of funds (though, in practice, her son would), allocate them to all the wards and monitor implementation.

The ward members would still remain Trishankus, but reaching for the high heavens of the mukhiyas seemed a little easier now.

In *A Single Man*, Sankarshan Thakur's singular biography of the man, there is a scene featuring a young Nitish Kumar in a coffee house. Still a college student and an aspiring neta, Kumar bangs the table with his fist and declares: '*Satta praapt karoonga, lekin satta leke achha kaam karoonga.*' (I shall get power by hook or by crook, but once I have got power, I will do good work.)

Over the years, Nitish Kumar himself has donned many roles: student, activist, leader, politician, Sushasan Babu, a fading hope for secular India and, more recently, alliance-hopper and power-seeker. If the seventy-year-old draws up a list of the 'achha kaam' he has pulled off in all his years as the most powerful man in Bihar, it ought to include his role as a democratiser of rural life—as a man who simultaneously amassed great power and sometimes shared it widely. It is undeniable that, through the twin policies of reservations and financial devolution, Kumar has managed to distribute power to socially and politically marginalised groups.

Nonetheless, these policies are very much works in progress. Take reservation for Dalits. We saw in Chapter 4 that a mountain of data supports the claim that reservation for Dalits has wrought successes. This is not immediately apparent, though. Many Dalit mukhiyas are still remote-controlled by the landed elite in villages. I know of a Yadav-dominated panchayat (not far from Patna) where a Yadav man married a Dalit widow only so he could become the de facto mukhiya when the panchayat was reserved for Dalit women. The brazenness of instances like these make them newsworthy, and they become part of the popular narrative. 'All reserved candidates are dummy candidates' is a complaint one often hears, expressed by everyone, from ordinary villagers to those in the highest echelons of government. There is, however, a more nuanced way of seeing this: the successes of reservation—borne out by the data—occur *despite* such problems, indicating that when, eventually, all Dalit mukhiyas are empowered enough to make their own decisions, the potential impacts could be much larger.

What then of decentralisation? The devolution of financial powers to ward members is an example of decentralisation at its purest: a real empowerment of the very lowest tiers of government. In one stroke, the successors of Circular No. 6278 had brought the local state closer to citizens' doorsteps. Where previously citizens could only hold the mukhiya—who lorded over 3,000 households—accountable for problems with local government, now they could rely on a more familiar face, one who represented a mere 225 households and was often from their own caste.

Decentralisation deepens democracy and gives voice to the marginalised. There are many scholars who will see that as an end in itself.

Others may ask: has this decentralisation resulted in better provision of public goods?

That question, as I see it, is moot. Bihar's rural landscape is poetry in shades of green. Previously, even in the more remote parts, modernity would be best epitomised by telephone towers that would stand like tall, chiselled, sentries, arms on hips. Now, in these past few years, one often sees a solitary circular water-tank resting on a fifteen-foot platform next to these towers (a stout Chacha Chaudhary next to the giant Sabu). Elsewhere, you will see a narrow drain riding alongside the road you are on; a brick-and-mud pathway branching off from the road to snake into a village; and inside these villages, taps and pipes to give the old chapakkals, or hand-pumps, company.

These are all the progeny of decentralisation, constructed through the Nal-Jal and Nali-Gali Yojanas.

The numbers bear this out: a whopping 2.3 lakh projects have been undertaken since 2017, as per administrative data. Over 95 per cent of wards across Bihar have undertaken at least one of a nali or a gali. And these are not 'ghost projects', assets that only exist in carefully managed government data. An audit we ran in 2018 across five districts found nearly all the assets mentioned in the government data.

And yet, the question is moot.

Take Mandesar Ram's case, a cautionary tale if there was ever one. Pipes and taps did not add up to running water. This is true of several such projects in densely packed, socially broken Bihar: they remain half-finished and mired in land disputes. Decentralisation can only get one so far. The combined powers of a Dalit ward member and a government-mandated decentralisation move can be overcome by nothing more than a bunch of scheming Bhumihar landlords.

Caste is, after all, an obstinate shape-shifter forever plaguing Indian society. But there is also another hierarchy to consider, one that is built into the structure of this executive-driven and court-circumscribed decentralisation move. This is the hierarchy of administration; one that not only positions mukhiyas above ward members, but also concentrates so much power in them—even after decentralisation—that they are a law unto themselves.

The twin hierarchies of caste and administration combine to sour the fruits of decentralisation. This was brought home to me all too clearly when I heard the recording of an interview with Kamal Manjhi, a ward member from Darbhanga. It was late one winter afternoon in Patna, as smog-stricken rays of the sun petered in through the large office windows of the ADRI, where I spent many happy days conducting research.

Kamal Manjhi is a Dalit, and his ward, comprising largely of Dalits was, high up in the pecking order for the implementation of the Nal-Jal Yojana, as per the rules. '*Mera* number *tha*, *mera* select *hona tha niyamanusaar*.' (It was my turn, my ward should have been selected for the projects as per the rules.) Manjhi's static-laden voice filled the office. '*Lekin mukhiya aur sevak milibhagat karke humko select nahin kiya gaya*.' (But the mukhiya and the secretary colluded to not select my ward.)

By telling Manjhi that his ward was not 'selected', the mukhiya—who was not a Dalit—was conjuring up excuses to not release funds for it. Money may or may not make the world go round, but it definitely allowed the mukhiyas to force their ward members make the rounds of government offices. The first claim on the state's money gave the mukhiyas more than a modicum of control over how things were run. The bargain was simple: 'You don't play by my rules, I won't release your funds.' These strictures were even harder to overcome when caste was thrown into the mix. Dalit ward members find themselves twice disadvantaged: socially by virtue of caste and administratively by virtue of their position.

It is not that the state was blind to these intertwining and potent hierarchies. Indeed, it is precisely for this reason that Circular No. 6278 mandated that Dalit ward members be given preference in allocation of projects.[93]

But those were mere rules mandated by the higher state.

Kamal Manjhi, however, was not quite done yet.

And, as I heard him recount his story—which we will see in full in the next chapter—on that hazy Patna afternoon, I remember being thrilled by how it panned out.

As a researcher who was training to be an academic, I knew I had stumbled upon something significant.

As someone who cared deeply about decentralisation and transparency in government, Manjhi's story seemed to open up a portal to another world.

---

[93] This is not entirely accurate. The rules mandate that wards with the maximum number of SCs and STs be given first preference. Once all such wards are exhausted, then, among the other wards, those with the highest population are served first and so on. Thus, all wards are covered over a three-year period. Now, as explained in this chapter, wards with a high number of SCs and STs almost always elect ward members who are also SCs. Bihar has very few STs (since most of the ST-majority areas in erstwhile Bihar are now in Jharkhand). Hence, SC ward members are usually the first to get access to these projects.

6

Apathy and a Shot at Redemption

A year of much change was 2014. In September, India launched Mangalyaan, a cube of five feet on each side that, to this day, traces elliptical patterns around Mars and churns out astonishing images. In October, an Indian and a Pakistani were jointly awarded the Nobel Peace Prize. Still, a historian chronicling twenty-first-century India a hundred years hence will perhaps only record an event from earlier in the year, when in May, the controversial Narendra Damodardas Modi was voted prime minister of the country. It was a moment that represented a discontinuity, a break in history, the dawn of a different India.

That very year, on 4 November, in front of the district collector's office in Muzaffarpur, a cry for a new India rang out. '*Naya zamaana–*' (A new era–), a man with a loudspeaker bellowed, '*aayega!*' (will emerge!), hundreds of voices responded in unison. '*Naya zamaana–*' he said once more, and the voices responded, even louder this time. The protestors were largely women. They were squeezed in together in the designated protest area, barely a few inches between them, the pallus of their sarees covering their heads. When the women raised their fists in unison, their bangles caught the gentle afternoon sun and glinted.

A banner tied to a tree and a wall read: '8.10.2014 *se anischitkaleen dharna*' (An indefinite strike from 8.10.2014). A smaller banner below it read: 'NREGA Bachao, NREGA Bachao' (Save NREGA, save NREGA). Fluttering flag-like, the highest banner of them all had four words painted in bright red: 'Samaj Parivartan Shakti Sangathan'. Above, on the same banner, but in smaller blue font was the motto: '*Hum jaanenge, hum jeeyenge*' (We will know, we will live).

SPSS mazdoors marked 4 November as the twenty-sixth day of the strike led by Sanjay Sahni. The mazdoors' main demand was that their wages be paid under the NREGA. They had worked for weeks and months together, creating tanks and bridges, lanes and gutters, only to see their bank accounts stay empty. Some had not been paid in over two years.

The dharna came at the end of a series of escalating complaints by the mazdoors: first, in person, to their local panchayat rozgar sevaks and mukhiyas; then to the BDO of their respective blocks; then, in the form of detailed letters, to the SDM; and finally, in the form of in-person meetings and letters, to the district authorities, including the district collector.

As the matter escalated, the mazdoors began to speak of going on strike, giving the state every opportunity to respond and prevent that eventuality. When the authorities continued to wring their hands, the strike was finally announced. This pattern of protest was in the best traditions of peaceful engagement with an unresponsive state, an art crafted by M.K. Gandhi in South Africa. In India, the Mahatma first piloted this strategy in Bihar (in villages around Motihari town, under 100 kilometres from Mahant Maniyari) during the Champaran struggles.

A century had passed since and a colonial state had been replaced by a democratically elected one. And yet, ironically, the state and its subjects found themselves falling into familiar patterns, an old dance between generational foes.

The protesting mazdoors of Muzaffarpur represented a tiny sliver of the state's subjects. Most others had nothing but hope to cling to, remaining stoic in the face of an apathetic state.

Apathy.

I used the word often to describe the Bihar government—and more broadly, the 'state'—in my initial months there. In an email to a friend, I wrote:

> The fact that the state—with its strange, feudal hierarchies, archaic filing systems and ad hoc mass transfers—still functions (even if sloppily) is a daily miracle. Many officers are only concerned with saving their backs, often resulting in a culture of apathy.

My bleak view of the state was shaped by an experience early in my stint in Bihar involving NREGA wage-payment delays. In September 2012, the state government ran out of NREGA funds. The Union government refused to release more funds until a substantial chunk of the existing expenditures were accounted for. In practice, this meant a massive record-reconciliation and data-entry exercise, involving thousands of mukhiyas, panchayat secretaries, BDOs and, most importantly, data-entry operators from across the state. This was an entirely avoidable problem, had some of this accounting been filed as funds were spent. Instead, over the first eight months of the year, the state spent as it willed and now, in the final quarter, it scrambled to record.

I saw all this play out as part of a research team that was to evaluate an electronic wage-payment system that the government was rolling out. This gave me a ring-side view of affairs. In another email documenting my experience, I wrote:

> In September 2012, Bihar ran out of money for the NREGA. The higher echelons of the state machinery barely registered the fact; the media couldn't care less. On the ground, the officers at the panchayat, block and district levels fretted, but didn't fume. The mazdoors whose payments had been held up expressed anguish, but weren't outraged. This was bizarre–for three whole months, the giant subsistence machine that is the NREGA abruptly stopped functioning–and no one seemed to really care.

I was perplexed, frustrated, aghast. By this time, I had met, and engaged with, NREGA mazdoors in Araria and Muzaffarpur. I found myself thinking of the women mazdoors of Muzaffarpur, who had taken buses and shared autos, braving rain and sun and an oppressive society that frowned upon any travel by women to show up at, and be inspired by, Sanjay's sabhas. How many months–or years–before they are paid for their work? I thought of the street-play I had recently witnessed in Araria, written and exuberantly performed by mazdoors. The play extolled the greatness of the NREGA, its abundant capacity to offer succour to the disadvantaged. For no fault of their own, the mazdoors and their play suddenly felt fake.

The state–or its members–can be cruel in different ways: through naked acts of violence (the murder of Ram Kumar Thakur); creative, and absurd, interpretations of the law (the judicial battle for reservations); even blatant displays of caste power (the story of Kamal Manjhi). In the end, these were acts of cruelty by *commission*: causing harm that is explicitly intended.

Living in Patna and travelling around Bihar in 2012, I was to witness another form of state cruelty: cruelty by *omission*. The state caused harm not intentionally, but because it could not be bothered enough.

One humid September afternoon, out in the field documenting causes for the delay in NREGA wage payments, I waited at a bus stand for a BDO.

Ten minutes later, a harried man with a small face and wearing thin-rimmed spectacles greeted me and introduced himself as the BDO. As we walked to his office, he explained how the internet was a huge problem in his south-Bihar town. He had a special broadband set up for his office, but somebody had cut the connecting wire ('*Kisi ne taar kat diya*'). He had now applied for a new connection and was waiting. His data-entry operator would get down to business as soon as the internet was back. Hopefully, this delay would not last too long, he told me, and the NREGA mazdoors would be paid soon.

We entered his office—a very large and slightly dank room—and I was greeted first by the sight of twenty or so angry men shouting down a petrified man (presumably another bureaucrat), a sight my companion took in with the equanimity of a priest in a confession box. We walked towards the BDO's desk, which lay at one corner of the room.

As we crossed the data entry operator's table, though, my eyes nearly popped out. In this apparently internet-starved office, the operator was by his laptop, watching a YouTube video featuring a skimpily clad blonde-haired woman and a car. I asked the BDO how the data entry operator was online—with a fast internet connection to boot (remember, this was 2012, an era dominated by 2G internet)—when he had just spent the past fifteen minutes spinning a tale of internet woes. '*Woh usska pi-rivate hai*' (That's his private connection), the BDO explained, pointing to the dongle that hung from the side of the laptop. 'I can't use that to get to him do government work.'

This, then, was the circular irony of the entire situation: the data entry operator at the block office watched videos on the internet while killing time waiting for the internet to arrive.

Mostly, though, the reasons have less to do with infrastructure (like the internet) and more to do with the design of the state. The state is byzantine, a complex system comprising several intertwining arms and layers. The NREGA required coordination across many of these arms. A single NREGA project could require the collaboration of officers across the Rural Development Department, the Panchayati Raj Department, the Public Health Engineering Department, the Postal Services and the Finance Department. Each department used to have a 'dialect' of its own, stemming from its own bureaucracy, filing systems and data protocols. Thus, when departments collaborated on projects, their systems had to learn to 'speak to each other'. This became a record-keeping nightmare, an optimisation problem with seemingly infinite constraints. The move to digital payment systems have helped solve *some* of these problems.

However, now as it was then, it does not help that nobody is ever in a hurry.

Thus, every eight or nine months, the system shuts down. No wages are paid. Projects are stalled. Everyone waits. Since it happens often, it is no longer seen as anathema, a crime against citizens. It is merely a glitch, a temporary and necessary pause. Everyone drinks their chais and watches YouTube videos to pass time.

This is the very definition of cruelty by omission.

This is apathy.

How does one right this systemic apathy? What institutional mechanisms can the state design to prevent itself from falling into lethargy?

In 2014, the protesting mazdoors of Muzaffarpur had some ideas. Tired of repeatedly complaining up the hierarchy, they wanted a one-stop shop for all their complaints; an autonomous arm of the state that would focus only on listening to the grievances of citizens and focus on redressing them. To this end, the SPSS issued a pamphlet in Hindi, signed by its members Sanjay Sahni, Santosh Thakur, Vinod Paswan, Lakhi Devi and Madina Begum. Translated to English, it read:

> Today the whole country is rocked by corruption. No work is done without bribes. Everyone has some complaint against the government, which no one is listening to. We keep going from this office to that office, but our complaint is rarely resolved in the right manner and on time. We need a grievance redressal law under which we can put forward our grievances and get them resolved in a timely manner. A *movement* has been started in Bihar on this issue, *which aims to implement the Grievance Redressal Act at the earliest.*

With this demand, SPSS claimed, the character of the protest had morphed, from strike, dharna, to movement, andolan.

Under a section titled 'How will this law come about?' the pamphlet read:

> The government is aware that in every corner of the state, lakhs of complaints against the government's workings are pending. Despite this, no institutional measures have been taken so far for their disposal. We all need to demand this law together so that the government can be put under pressure and this law can be brought at the earliest.

The memories of the Lokpal movement were still fresh. On the back of that movement, Arvind Kejriwal had miraculously become chief minister of Delhi. SPSS's demands for a grievance redressal law may have been influenced by Kejriwal's successes. But its demand for an autonomous body of individuals at different levels as opposed to an all-powerful Lokpal was in line with the position of many eminent scholars and activists who privileged the institution over an individual.

There was one clear way in which Anna Hazare's Lokpal movement had left its mark: the protestors assembled outside the collector's office wore pristine white Nehru topis, à la Anna's supporters.[94]

A week may be a long time in politics, but eighteen months can be a blip in an administrative timeline. Nevertheless, eighteen months after the Muzaffarpur protests, the Bihar Right to Public Grievance Redressal Act (BPGRA, as it is referred to, rather than BRPGRA) was passed and a state-wide grievance redressal platform was launched. It is unlikely that the Muzaffarpur strike had anything to do with the Act being passed. The strike was called off in November 2014 on the back of a significant chunk of the wage dues being cleared. Subsequently, the mazdoors made sporadic demands for a grievance redressal mechanism, but nothing potent enough to jolt the state into action.

The seeds of the grievance redressal law were sown elsewhere. A decade previously, in his first term as chief minister, Nitish Kumar had initiated Janata Darbars or 'People's Courts'. District

---

94 The Anna Movement famously had the words 'Main Anna Hoon' printed on its Nehru topis. On the other hand, the Muzaffarpur protestors went with 'Samaj Parivartan Shakti Sangathan'. In doing so, the mazdoors were making it clear that the movement privileged the collective over the individual.

collectors from across the state were asked to throw open their doors to the public once a week. Anybody could walk in and complain. Most would complain about errant local officials causing problems: an unissued ration card, a non-existent road, an unfiled FIR, an unauthorised land transaction.

I once happened to be in the Collectorate office in Gaya on the day of the darbar. I was struck by the long line of patiently waiting persons, their diverse sartorial choices—chequered shirts, white dhotis, gamchhas and the odd turbans, sarees, monkey-caps and shawls—indicative of their wide-ranging social standings. To say that the darbars were popular would be an understatement.

Far more popular than the collectors' darbars were the ones conducted by the chief minister himself. Within four months of taking over, Nitish Kumar launched Janata Ke Darbar Mein Mukhyamantri (the chief minister in the people's court). Every week, the chief minister's official residence in Patna would function as a darbar, where he would welcome petitioners and complainants. The janata may have still had to trudge to Patna to be at 'their' darbar, but Nitish Kumar left no stone unturned in giving them a hearing. The political scientist Rohan Mukherjee, who spent some time in Patna in 2009, noted:[95]

> Senior government officials had to be present with the chief minister at these events in order to note specific complaints. Complaints were assigned unique numbers that complainants could use to track progress on their cases. The Darbar became a regular fixture in the chief minister's schedule, and citizens came from all over Bihar to submit grievances.

---

[95] Rohan Mukherjee, 'Reviving the Administration: Bihar State, India, 2005–2009', Innovations for Successful Societies, Princeton University, 2009, https://successfulsocieties.princeton.edu/sites/successfulsocieties/files/Policy_Note_ID115.txt.

Subsequently, in January 2009, the chief minister decided to hold his darbar among the people. Mukherjee notes that he 'replicated the darbar model at the village level. At these meetings, Kumar was known to give out the cellphone numbers of senior government officials, including the chief secretary of the state administration, to citizens so that they could follow up on their petitions'.

By 2016, Kumar had held 241 darbars—averaging roughly one every two weeks—and heard 2,77,249 complaints.

Not everyone was impressed with Nitish Kumar's Anil Kapoor-in-*Nayak* turn.[96] One activist noted:

> Watching the Chief Minister's Janata Darbar is like watching a monarch. You can't just make orders like that. This is all just a kind of drama. The Chief Minister can't solve land disputes. He can't solve criminal cases. Only a court can. He can't suspend an official. He can only recommend it to his superior. If we lived in a kingdom then the Chief Minister could solve these problems, but we live in a society with the rule of law.

Kumar, a politician who thought like a bureaucrat, was aware of these issues. He commissioned a group of retired Bihar Administrative Service (BAS) officers to work as 'grievance redress officers', whose job was to follow up on complaints made at these darbars. The officers forwarded the grievances to relevant arms of the state, tracked actions taken by local bureaucrats and reported back to complainants.

Despite this, the system lacked teeth. As one scholar noted: '[T]he grievance redress officers have the power to penalize other

[96] In the movie *Nayak: The Real Hero* (2001), Anil Kapoor becomes chief minister for a day and walks around with his secretary and a type-writer, solving people's problems in real time.

officials, but do so rarely, perhaps because they pride themselves on working with officials rather than acting as adversaries or, perhaps, because, as former bureaucrats themselves, they are reluctant to become confrontational with their former colleagues.'[97]

The protesting mazdoors of Muzaffarpur knew the current mechanism was insipid. Hence, they demanded a new grievance redressal law that set up an 'institutional framework' which 'resolved citizens' complaints in a timely manner'.

Surprisingly, they found a kindred spirit in no less than the chief minister of Bihar. Addressing a gathering at the Sri Krishna Memorial Hall in Patna's historic Gandhi Maidan, Nitish Kumar said in 2016: 'On the basis of my experience of holding Janata Darbar meetings for ten years, I can say people got the opportunity to be heard at police stations, blocks, districts and state headquarters. But there was no guarantee of their grievances being redressed. Most of the grievances remained unresolved and that used to haunt my mind.'[98]

These words were uttered on 5 June 2016, the day the new Bihar Right to Public Grievance Redressal Act—or, its equally official-sounding Hindi title, Bihar Lok Shikayat Nivaran Adhikar Adhiniyam—was launched. Under the law, 101 new grievance redressal officers, each endowed with dedicated staff and office, were appointed across the state.

---

[97] Nick Robinson, 'Complaining to the State: Grievance Redress and India's Social Welfare Programs', CASI Working Paper Series, 2013, p. 20.

[98] PTI, 'Nitish launches Public Grievance Redressal Act in Bihar', *Busines Standard*, https://www.business-standard.com/article/pti-stories/nitish-launches-public-grievance-redressal-act-in-bihar-116060500638_1.html.

These new officers differed from their predecessors under the old system in four ways: first, they were not retired bureaucrats, but represented the best and the brightest among currently serving BAS officers, handpicked by the Chief Minister's Office; second, in addition to attempting to resolve complaints made at the various darbars, these officers invited citizens to complain directly to them; third, the new officers were not merely tracking complaints, they were tasked with holding 'hearings' featuring the complainant and the relevant departmental bureaucrat against whom the complaint was made.

However, the fourth, and most important, difference had nothing to do with the operational elements of the grievance redressal system. It was enshrined in how the law chose to see grievance redressal—not as something the state deigned to do, condescending to bestow its largesse on the masses, but as something citizens had every right (adhikar) to demand. The law bestowed every citizen with a right to redressal of their complaint within sixty days of making it.

Bihar was the first state in the country—and, as of writing this chapter, the only one—that made grievance redressal a right. This right nested the following rights: a right to file their complaint for free, a right to facilitation of the complaint, a right to information regarding the complaint, a right to receipt of a tracking number, a right to hearings, a right to redress and, finally, even a right to appeal. This marked a shift in how the officers viewed their roles: they were not doing citizens a favour by solving their problems, but were doing right by the law.

BPGRA was, then, a shot at redemption.

An apathetic state wanted citizens to tell it stories of its own apathy, promising not to mock, but to listen and make amends.

Within months of the Act being launched in 2016, I visited the Subdivisional Public Grievance Redressal Office in Patna, located in Patna's Collectorate complex.

I was there to meet Seema Kumari, the public grievance redressal officer (PGRO). Her office was small and windowless, comprising a table, a few chairs and a low drawer against a wall that housed brown browbeaten government files. Two white tube-lights were the only sources of light and a ceiling fan whirred noisily above. A door at the back of the room led to a tiny anteroom where some of her staff (young men who could operate computers and type quickly) sat.

Kumari sat on one side of the table. Facing her were two gentlemen, the circle officer and a lackey from the Patna Sadar Police Station. I was seated on a hastily drawn chair along the third side of the table. It was an overcast Thursday. Thursdays, overcast or not, were reserved for police-related hearings, and there were thirty-six hearings to be conducted on the day I visited.

I witnessed a hearing regarding a missing child. The complainant—the child's father—claimed that the police had refused to file an FIR in the matter. The circle officer produced documentary evidence to show that an FIR had, in fact, been filed. The police were now investigating the matter. After ensuring the papers were in order (while the circle officer answered phone calls from the local thana, police station) Kumari marked the complaint 'resolved'.

Remarkably, throughout all this, the complainant was absent.

'The law is clear,' Kumari told me by way of explanation. 'We are to hold hearings irrespective of the presence of the complainant.'

The state, when moulded in Seema Kumari's image, was effortlessly efficient.

When I visited Muzaffarpur a week later, the state manifested differently. Manoj Kumar, the PGRO, exuded an air of self-importance typical of many male bureaucrats. Garrulous by nature and eager to impress, he reminded me of the Indian uncle who speaks in idioms and clichés and makes grand pronouncements, all with an arm around your shoulder.

Befitting his personality, the officer's hearings were grand affairs in a sprawling replica of a courtroom. Manoj Kumar sat in the judge's box; the complainant and the local bureaucrat had their own stands on either side. Row upon row of seats formed the viewers' gallery.

The complaint up for hearing pertained to mismanagement of the village high school by the headmaster. This was, much to my surprise, the tenth and final hearing. Manoj Kumar let both parties state their positions, which they did in a long-winded way, interrupting each other like squabbling siblings. Adopting an officious tone, he then posed a series of rambling queries. Everyone treated time with the nonchalance of saints. Much of this was performance, likely for the sake of us visitors from Patna. But how much of it?

I quickly lost interest and stared around. Besides us, the two researchers from Patna, there were a few others in the visiting gallery, mostly complainants waiting their turn. The PGRO's staff, including a peon and the IT manager, stood by the door, watching proceedings between glances at their phones. A few hangers-on lingered, men whose presence is both inexplicable and customary in every bureaucratic space in India.

At some point, a shabby, weary, middle-aged man walked into the room asking for justice. He was a former complainant. He had previously filed a grievance that nobody had shown up in his village to measure his lands. Back then, Manoj Kumar had ordered the local amin, land surveyor, to survey the man's lands and make measurements. The amin obliged and Kumar marked the complaint 'resolved'. An order was passed.

The complainant, however, was still unhappy. He felt the amin had made a mistake: some part of his land was left unaccounted for. And so, that morning, he burst into the courtroom, asking for insaaf, justice. '*Aap* appeal *file keejiye*' (Please file an appeal), one of the staff told the man, ushering him out.

That was our only source of entertainment in a hearing with no end in sight. Over an hour had passed. Manoj Kumar was still peering at the two parties over his glasses, still interpreting—and sometimes merely restating—facts, still behaving like a cross between an investigator and a professor. I joked to the IT manager, who was now sitting beside me, that the two parties seemed to be old foes. Much to my surprise, he responded: '*Arey, ye ek chacha–bhatija ka hi jhagda maaniye aap!*' (Oh yes, think of this as a fight between an uncle and his nephew!) The school-management issue, he proceeded to explain, was merely a new front for an old family feud between the two gentlemen, a fact known to everyone involved. What a tremendous waste of the state's resources, I thought.

By the time Manoj Kumar pronounced his judgement, I was exhausted. The BPGRA, in Kumar's hands, felt less like a right and more like a tiring act.

Kamal Manjhi, the Dalit ward member from Darbhanga we encountered in the previous chapter, was in a quandary. He was a ward member, an elected representative. Yet, no one—not the mukhiya, who was not a Dalit, nor the BDO, nor the district officials—seemed to pay much heed to his concerns. The mukhiya simply refused to release funds to implement piped-water projects in Manjhi's ward.

Desperate for some relief, Manjhi decided to complain *against* the state. It was only recently he had heard of the BPGRA or, as it was colloquially known, Jan Shikayat (literally, 'People's Complaint'). Manjhi, being a member of the local state himself, was no ordinary 'jan'. He was a ward member, an officer of the state. Nevertheless, Manjhi decided to file a complaint against the local state. To do this, he took two buses to reach the subdivisional headquarters, stood in the queue like every aam aadmi, common man, with a grievance in front of the Jan Shikayat office.

Once his complaint was filed, he waited.

Within weeks, Manjhi was called for the first of three hearings. He took those two buses once more and landed up at the grievance redressal office. Manjhi met with the grievance redressal officer and explained his predicament. The officer listened patiently and said he would be called again.

The call duly came, and this time around, Manjhi entered the public grievance officer's chamber to find himself face-to-face with his adversaries, the mukhiya and the BDO. '*Sabke saamne humne poora samasya bataaya*' (I explained the whole situation in front of everyone), Manjhi said. The grievance redressal officer listened to his impassioned pleas and his opponents' responses. He asked them all to come back in a few weeks' time.

On the occasion of third and final hearing, the grievance redressal officer read out his order in the presence of both parties. The order, written in stiff officialese, mandated that the mukhiya and the BDO transfer funds to Manjhi's ward. In Manjhi's words, this was akin to a chain reaction: 'When the BDO was pressurised by the officer, he, in turn, pressurised the mukhiya and money was transferred to my ward.'

In weeks, his ward, comprising the poorest and most discriminated households, saw water gushing through freshly laid pipes and new drains being built.

It was a glorious incongruity: a member of the state had repurposed a citizen's forum to make one arm of the state twist another into action.

In describing his experiences, Manjhi saved his best words for the grievance redressal officer: 'He was an extremely nice man, not too old. Maybe in his forties. I went with a specific request and the system–and this officer, in particular–really helped me ... I am very impressed with the system. I don't remember the officer's full name, but he was some Jha.' The Jhas are Maithil Brahmins, among the most privileged castes in Bihar.

The grievance redressal system had allowed the Dalit ward member Manjhi to transcend not merely administrative hierarchies, but also that of caste, in more ways than one.

Over 8.5 lakh complaints have been filed under the BPGRA since its launch in 2016. These complaints have spawned across forty-four bureaucratic departments, spanning virtually every aspect of government functioning.

The complainants were diverse, their grievances ranging from the mundane to the grave: a certain Pathak, a Brahmin from Patna, complained about squatters. It was bad enough that their jhopdis, huts, encroached upon public roads, Pathak said, but worse still, his puritanical sensibilities were offended by their public consumption of meat. Kavi Ranjan, a Dalit youth from Bhojpur, complained about a common problem in this era of digital transfers: data-entry errors. His post-matriculation scholarship was transferred to the wrong bank account, one that differed from his by a single digit. Deep Narayan Paswan complained that the mukhiya of his village had released only half the funds allocated under a scheme to help BPL families conduct funerals. A woman I spoke to had complained that she lost her young son to a freak accident featuring a dangling live wire. She wanted compensation.

In 2018, we ran a survey of 1,047 randomly sampled complainants from across Bihar. A third of the complainants said their grievances had been resolved. Curiously, many more—close to 75 per cent of the respondents—were satisfied with the BPGRA, rating their experience as either 'good', 'very good' or 'excellent'. As one complainant told us: 'The BDO was forced to come and speak with us at the hearing and he was even scolded by the grievance redressal officer in front of me! My complaint was not fully resolved. And I know the two of them—the BDO and the grievance redressal officer—may go and have chai afterwards, but I was very satisfied with the entire experience.'

An apathetic state had put on a gentler face and listened. This intent was reflected elsewhere too: when I had gone to meet Seema Kumari, the grievance redressal officer in Patna, I was surprised by the unusually large, bright hoardings beckoning passers-by. They announced that one was in the vicinity of a grievance redressal office and walked readers through the process of filing complaints.

As I entered the office complex, I saw two orderly queues outside: one was to register complaints; the second, equally long one, was for a window that asked: 'May I Help You?' The counter's main function was to help complainants convert their verbal complaints into written ones. More strangely for a government office–where waiting and standing usually went hand in hand–there were seats for complainants to sit in while they awaited their turn.

The state had listened, and had even gone a little further: it had also begun to make amends. A third–33 per cent–of the complaints being redressed may seem like a small number, but it compares favourably with other contexts from around the world. It is also a remarkable achievement for a state like Bihar, where, even fifteen years ago, the bureaucracy was entirely emaciated, the state was in the midst of a crisis of law and order and incapable of spending its own resources.

Despite all the positives, to say that the BPGRA works as it should would be far from the truth. Awareness about the system remains low, despite the government's best efforts. A survey of BPL card holders in 2017 said that fewer than 5 per cent of households had heard of the mechanism. A more recent survey we conducted in 2019 suggested that only a quarter of ward members could answer basic questions about it.

How do we still have 8.5 lakh complaints filed under the Act? That number is deceptive: it translates to around five complaints per day per grievance redressal office. Only 2.5 per cent of Bihar's approximately 30 million households have ever filed a complaint.

What is more, things do not look like they are improving either: the number of incoming complaints has mostly stagnated.

Why is this the case?

Filing complaints and attending hearings is costly. There is one grievance redressal office for every 450 villages. Kamal Manjhi took two buses to reach the grievance redressal centre to file his complaint. Subsequently, he was asked to attend three hearings. Four trips, sixteen bus rides, an entire working week was placed at the altar of the grievance redressal mechanism. Our estimates suggest it costs 75 per cent of the daily minimum wage to travel and attend a hearing. Manjhi was a public official: delivering piped water was central to his job. What of the woman mazdoor whose few days of work in a month clashes with the schedule of the hearings? What of the eighty-year-old, cataract-eyed Gobind Sah (whom we encountered in Chapter 3) who was not issued a BPL card?

To be fair to the makers of the Act, showing up at the grievance redressal office is not necessary. Complaints can be filed remotely—through the phone, via the internet or even through post. And as Seema Kumari told me, the grievance redressal officer must conduct hearings even in the absence of the complainant. In such cases, the grievance redressal officer acts as both lawyer for the complainant *and* judge.

Yet, the overwhelming majority of complaints—over 75 per cent—are filed in person. The reasons are many. Internet literacy is low. Phone-in complainants are still rare, partly because the call centre in Patna is staffed with unenthusiastic urban youth. How do we know this? Because we actually tried to test how efficient the call centre was. To do so, we used 'mystery shoppers', a technique commonly deployed to conduct audits. We trained enumerators to act as complainants and call up the call centre.[99] Fifty calls were made. The results confirmed

[99] The enumerators did not actually file their fictitious complaints through the call centre youth. They merely stopped at asking if the call centre staff were willing to file a complaint on their behalf. If the staff member agreed, then the enumerator replied that they would call back at a later point and never followed up.

our hunch that those manning the call centre were merely whiling away time: only a third of our calls resulted in successful attempts to file complaints. The rest of the time, the calls went unanswered. When they were answered, in classic bureaucratic style, the receiver asked the caller to visit their nearest grievance redressal centre in person (thereby defeating the very purpose of the call). In other instances, the enumerator was asked to call back at a later time.

What about hearings, then? Can the complainant skip them and save some money? Surveys showed that redressal rates plummet when the complainants do not show up. Clearly, not all grievance redressal officers followed Seema Kumari's dual-role dictum of playing judge and lawyer for absentee complainants.

Thus, many of the poorest–and more marginalised–find themselves edged out of the system. The data bears this out: women, Dalits, the illiterate, old and the infirm are all under-represented. The further a village is from the grievance redressal office, the lower its contribution to the overall pool of complaints. Ironically, these villages are poorer and rely more heavily on the state for sustenance.[100]

---

100 When people do complain, they end up complaining about a really big problem: a disputed plot of land, large discrepancies in land taxes levied, a missing family member. The data on complaints show that land and police-related matters form nearly 40 per cent of all complaints filed. This is when a third of the households in rural Bihar do not even own any land. Police apathy is rarely an individual's main grievance, even for the mazdoors of Muzaffarpur who regularly clash with the local state. Indeed, the state is more directly manifested in the mukhiya and the ward members, the vikas mitra and the anganwadi sevika. (A vikas mitra is a member of the Mahadalit community who is an 'agent of change' and acts as a bridge between the government and Mahadalit families, helping them access government benefits. An anganwadi sevika co-runs the angandwadi, a key rural childcare centre.) Yet, complaints regarding housing, rations, pensions, healthcare benefits—issues that plague the disadvantaged—are less likely to reach the state's ears.

The voices of the most oppressed and desperate are thus lost. In its commitment to listening, the state seemed to have overlooked the basic truism that to listen, one must first *hear*.

These negatives should not distract from the promise of the BPGRA. On paper, like the NREGA, it is a stellar Act, crafted to empower and endowed with immense potential.

The summer of 2019 gave us a glimpse of how this could come to be.

Only months earlier, I had encountered Kamal Manjhi's story through a recording at the ADRI. Two voices had filled the room: one was Manjhi's own, the interviewee; the other was his interrogator, Chanchal Kumar Singh, my co-researcher of almost a decade by this time. Chanchal is, depending on which official document you rely on (and who among his three younger siblings you ask), either twenty-eight, thirty or thirty-two. He is short and blessed with lean limbs, though he has nurtured a fatherly paunch in recent years.

I went to Chanchal when I first noticed patterns in the complaints data that pointed to the fact that ward members were repurposing BPGRA to complain against the local state. Chanchal, Bhanu Shikha (another young researcher) and I designed a short survey to investigate the matter. Our team of enumerators, housed in the IDFC Institute's Patna office, spoke to a sample of ward members from across the state who had complained. This is how we chanced upon Kamal Manjhi. His story pointed us to a potent mixing of what we had thus far been studying as somewhat separate elements: decentralisation, caste and BPGRA.

Manjhi's was a remarkable story. But was he alone?

Once more, Chanchal and I worked together. We went about looking for data on Nal-Jal and Nali-Gali Yojanas. We tracked down a public dataset—languishing in the backwaters of the internet—that displayed all the 98,000 lanes, drains and piped-water projects built under the schemes. I analysed the data to first establish that Manjhi was not alone: Dalit ward members were systematically discriminated against by upper-caste mukhiyas. Projects were delayed: in the first year of the scheme, Dalit wards got 29 per cent fewer projects in panchayats where the mukhiya was a non-Dalit.

Did everyone turn to the BPGRA for recourse? It turned out that, in this regard, Manjhi was an outlier, a statistical anomaly. Only a vanishing fraction—a mere 2 per cent—of Bihar's 20,000-odd Dalit ward members had filed a complaint. We had some sense of why this may be the case: to begin with, most ward members did not know the BPGRA existed. However, even when they did know, many were unwilling to bear the high costs of complaining and travelling for hearings. Still others, having been at the receiving end of a hierarchical society's lack of concern for many years, felt that the system would not work in their favour.

Could we make it easier for Dalit ward members to complain? Would that systematically improve project implementation? Or was Manjhi's case a one-off, a fluke, a product of the stars aligning perfectly?

We tested this by running a large randomised controlled trial. Chanchal and Bhanu Shikha led a team of enumerators based out of Patna. The enumerators contacted Dalit ward members from across the state over the phone and offered to file complaints on their behalf. This was the summer of 2019, over two years after the Nal-Jal and Nali-Gali Yojanas had been handed over to the ward members. Yet, there were, as per official data, about 5,000 Dalit wards that had not implemented these projects.

The study covered 1,629 Dalit ward members from every one of Bihar's thirty-eight districts. Roughly half of these were randomised to a 'treatment' group and the rest were part of the 'control' group. We offered to file complaints on behalf of those who were randomised to the treatment group. Of ward members in this treatment group, 41 per cent accepted our offer. Evidently, once ward members were told about the BPGRA, many were enthusiastic about complaining.

Over the next few months, the stories began to trickle in. One ward member said that the mukhiya had shown up at his doorstep on the day of the first hearing and asked him to withdraw the complaint. When asked why, the mukhiya responded by saying that he had transferred the money to the ward member's bank account that very morning.

Another ward member had refused our offer to file a complaint on his behalf when we had contacted him. When we spoke to him months later, he said something even more startling. After our enumerator had spoken to him, he walked up to the mukhiya's house and threatened to file a complaint. 'I know someone in Patna who will file a complaint for me,' he said. That was all it took: the very next day, the mukhiya had signed all the approvals and asked him to hire a contractor and lay a pipe.

Some stories had a tinge of humour. A certain Kedar Ram called up furiously to note that his name had been wrongly recorded in the complaint. Our enumerator, who failed to pick up his first name over the din of background noise and static, had entered her best guess: 'Betaal Ram'. Betaal is, of course, a legendary vampire in Hindu mythology. On being ushered into the hearing, the grievance redressal officer greeted Ram with the words: 'Namaste, Betaal-ji.' Ram was shocked and minced no words with our enumerator on a call later that day: '*Sunwai achha gaya, lekin bhoot bana diya aap ne humko!*' (The hearing went fine, but you have turned me into a ghost!)

Four months after the complaints were filed, we recontacted the 1,629 ward members as part of our endline survey (another sprawling survey exercise conducted under the aegis of Chinmaya Kumar and another researcher, Manasi Rao). The results were unambiguous, corroborating our accounts from the field. Dalit ward members in the treated group were 26 per cent likelier to have projects initiated in their wards when compared to those in the control group. The grievance redressal system had forced the mukhiyas to release funds and cooperate with their ward members.

Kamal Manjhi, thus, was not an outlier, but an exemplar of the potential encompassed within the BPGRA.

Sometimes, travelling across villages in Bihar, one gets the impression that the state is omnipresent, the very ocean in which society swims. The state is in the little ziplock bag people bring out when you go to survey their households, containing all their state-mandated ID cards; in the stained and oversized uniform of the little child savouring mud by her thatched home; in the wall paintings promoting the cycle scheme for girls; on the foundation stones littered across the rural landscape for various government projects, a road, a drain, a flagpost in a school ground; in the roof of a newly built home that owes its existence to the second instalment of the housing scheme, the Pradhan Mantri Awas Yojana; on that poster for yet another coaching class to crack the BAS entrance exam. In the Naxal-affected villages of Imamganj in Gaya, it is in the solitary, armed CRPF jawan amusing himself by kicking a stone around aimlessly. And finally, the state is present as individuals who represent it: the vikas mitra, the tola sevak, the anganwadi sevika, the ASHA worker, the ward member, the school teacher, the mukhiya.

The BPGRA, flaws and all, has the potential to keep tabs on many of these facets of the state. Yet, for the most part, the Act is a patch, a temporary fix on individual, infinitesimal and immediate problems. The state is a giant, complex machine and the BPGRA is the mechanic.[101] A mechanic can keep things going, but she cannot redesign the machine, or finance new parts, or design incentives to make employees work efficiently.

Similarly, the BPGRA offers a recourse for redressing individual acts of apathy—and less frequently, cruelty—by the state, but it cannot solve deeper, structural issues. It cannot tackle the lack of resources to fund education and healthcare overhauls. Nor can it develop a vision for revamping the failing judicial system, or take on the normalisation of corruption in daily life. It cannot implement in letter and spirit, all considerations be damned, the rights-based laws the state had promulgated and passed over the past two decades.

Yet, in a sense, it was the limited radicalism of the Act that contributed to its successes. The BPGRA made it possible for one arm of the state to oversee other arms, without ever threatening their existence. On being summoned to the grievance redressal officer's hearings, the local bureaucrat grumbled but rarely protested. The number of complaints were

---

[101] As, indeed, are the other transparency-inducing measures, such as the Right to Public Services Act or the Right to Information Act, or even social audit mechanisms.

nearly always manageable, the questions being asked of local bureaucrats were pointed, but not so sharp as to maim anyone. The boat wobbled, but did not rock. The grievance redressal officer was an irritant but never an enemy.

On the face of it, there were two reasons why the mazdoors of Muzaffarpur, who had so vociferously demanded a powerful grievance redressal system, quickly grew disillusioned with the BPGRA. Firstly, within a year of being in force, the NREGA was removed from the ambit of the Act. This was because the scheme, which was centrally mandated, already had a provision for a Lokpal under Section 27 of the National Rural Employment Guarantee Act.

Besides, the mazdoors had carefully weighed the costs and benefits of the BPGRA: the flicker of a promise of redressal was simply not worth expending all those resources complaining and attending hearings.

Beyond these two reasons was a third, more important one: the limited radicalism of the BPGRA simply could not contain the mazdoors' more substantive vision for how the state should function.

They wanted more. The mazdoors wanted the state to change its ways, to not merely listen and make small amends, but show remorse and redeem itself. They did not simply want the NREGA to function such that the mazdoors got *some* work, they wanted a full 100 days of work on demand, and unemployment benefits if they were denied such work. They were not satisfied with roads being built in their villages; they sent teams of women mazdoors out–armed with glasses of sattu juice–to stand in the searing heat and monitor *how* these roads were being constructed, what kind of material was being used and whether the labour was locally hired or not.

The mazdoors, and Sanjay Sahni himself, had begun to realise that the avenues for change they pursued were simply too narrow to accommodate the breadth of their dreams.

In July 2019, as Chanchal and I and the rest of the Patna team were designing the endline survey for the Kamal Manjhi-inspired randomised controlled trial, I called Sanjay to say I was coming to his village to take a break. It had been a while since I had seen him, a Ratnauli visit was overdue.

It was on this phone call that, for the first time, he let slip in conversation that an idea had begun to form in his mind.

The Assembly elections of 2020, he reminded me, were a year-and-a-half away. He said:

'*Hum ladenge.*' (I will contest.)

7

The Stories We Tell

Muzaffarpur, June 2019

It is hot. Forty-three degrees Celsius is not so bad when you know there is no AC around the corner. You adapt, life moves on. Things get hot when life is still. Or when one is on a chair in a room with a thatched roof on a breeze-free afternoon, nodding off after delicious egg-curry for lunch, but is rudely awoken by the ... heat. This is how it was with our taxi driver who later took his cab and ran away to Patna, most likely because he realised the heat was not going anywhere. '*Kitni garmi hai*,' he says, stating the obvious as he angles for sympathy, and wipes sweat-beads clean with a hand-towel.

The heat is everywhere, but that barely stops anyone from working. At 11 a.m., in our car, we arrive at a village called Kishunpur Balram, where about fifty women (and maybe two men and three under-eighteen youngsters) are clearing the canal, shovel in hand, charting a path for a rain-fed river to traverse. This is a worksite under the NREGA. The earth is yellow, the leaves are dust-layered, the soil cracked. A person who did not know any better would scoff at the optimism—a river, through this parched earth?

Sanjay Sahni asks the women to gather around for a short meeting (pronounced 'mitting', which always reminds me of 'mitti' and 'mitti ka kaam', working on clearing the earth—the kind of work most NREGA labourers do).

Issues are discussed, fault lines appear. Someone complains about how not everyone comes on time. The agreed-upon work hours are 6 a.m. to 12 p.m. The hours seem intense; even more so if you are, like many of these women, in your forties, fifties or sixties. Gruelling physical work—swoop-hack-shovel, swoop-hack-shovel—and all for a sum of Rs 30 per hour. Someone else complains about teenage children substituting for workers. A burst of allegations and counter-allegations follows. Ever the schoolteacher, Sanjay shouts some people down, encourages others to speak up, restores some semblance of order and then, slowly, says:

'I hope you have heard the news ...'

This is the news: Sanjay Sahni—who has fought for the rights of mazdoors for most of this decade, with some degree of success and at great personal cost (including nine false cases, some criminal, some administrative, registered against him)—now wants to raise the stakes. He is contesting the 2020 Assembly elections in Bihar, from Muzaffarpur's Kurhani constituency.

The women have heard the news. Their response is one of considerable enthusiasm. We need a mazdoor on the inside, they say, echoing Sanjay's words. The choice of word, 'inside' or 'andar', for being in power is instructive. The incumbent prime minister of India, that most insider of insiders, rode to power twice claiming to be an outsider. If he is an outsider, these mazdoors are from Mars, separated from the inside by a vast expanse of darkness. The system is technically democratic, and, on paper, everyone can rocket into it from their respective orbits. Or, at the very least, have their finest take the ticket to the inside. 'But when was the last time a mazdoor was on the inside?' Sanjay asks. More affirmative nods, some distracted chatter.

We leave soon after, because we, quite literally, have miles to travel. More bodies toiling in the relentless heat, more warm welcomes, more zindabads, more talk of job cards and daily kaam. Also, more knowing smiles about 'the news', more excitement about the man on the inside, more conjuring of plastic glasses and offers of cold drink (Thums Up or Sprite), more invitations to lunch declined, more squabbling, more cross-talking and more–much more–sun.

Every time the speech is just a little different. Mostly, he begins with what the ideal daily wage should be. It is Rs 180 now. Should it be raised to 250? 300? Why not 500? One variation throws in a sarcastic zinger: 'This year, the government raised the NREGA wage by a princely sum of 3 rupees'. Sometimes he is cagey about telling them he is all in–he wants it to come from them. '*Zara aap bhi charcha keejiye*,' he says. Discuss among yourselves. Should we not have one of us on the inside? Sometimes he talks of the broken schooling system, of a masterji who, even when he does show up, does nothing.

In his last speech for the day, he brings up the public healthcare crisis. He corrects someone when they suggest that a primary health centre's only job is to dispense polio drops. In the midst of some chatter, one woman mentions in passing the deadly fever that affects babies: the children fall ill and they are gone. Her face registers pain momentarily. Sanjay, meanwhile, has moved on: he is telling someone else that a job card is what you call a labour card in English. In all this somewhat disorienting chaos, the only constant is Sanjay's buzzing phone. On nearly every occasion, he stops speaking to answer the call, telling the caller he is busy and assuring them he would attend to them later.

In the afternoon, after the egg curry, we see Sanjay work his craft. Two women show up from Marwan, about 30 kilometres away. There is an ongoing NREGA worksite in their panchayat, but the women have been denied access. Like a doctor enquiring about the patient's history, he shoots off a bunch of queries: do you have a job card? Is your name on the muster roll? Do you know any of the others who are working on the same muster roll? He learns their names. Once he has diagnosed the issue, he educates them about the NREGA–a few, quick practical pointers on how to negotiate with the mukhiya and the PRS, the BDO and the bank manager. He then checks some records on the NREGA website. Next, calls are made to various government offices and, in about half an hour, a cure is found. He has worked the system and the two women's names have been added to the muster rolls. They can report to the worksite the very next day.

This is it, then: ten years of learning-by-doing distilled into a forty-five-minute masterclass.

And yet, an election is a whole different beast. In the afternoon, when the sun is too hot for us to visit villages, I attempt to grill him in the office. The reason there is no mazdoor on the inside, I argue, is not for want of trying: money, party, status, planning and strategy all play key parts, and are loaded in favour of the insiders. Has he considered the repercussions that contesting would have on the movement, his work, his saathis, even himself? Give me three months, he says, and we will get the word around: every mazdoor will bring four votes. 'What if you lose?' I ask. Here, he hesitates and then gives me a weird two-part answer. First, he won't lose. Second, if he does, he will go back to the movement. Even if he does not mention it, I notice that all this talk of campaigning for elections has made him actively work towards expanding his base, something that augurs well for the movement too.

Before the four-hour return in a bus packed with sweat-bathed students, a moment of glorious respite: we are on a battery-operated rickshaw on the highway—a silent, whirring tortoise among lumbering, louder beasts—riding a gentle breeze. On the outskirts of Muzaffarpur, the landscape is dark, with lights from the odd home floating past us. I stretch my legs and it feels like 1996, and we are on the sleeper-class berth looking out the window as the darkness flies past. Sanjay Sahni's story is the odd light shining bright in the dizzying darkness—only time will tell if the infinitesimal chance of it exploding into a new dawn materialises.

Political success is often bequeathed. Indian politics is famously littered with dynasts. That, however, does not stop many without a recognisable surname from trying. Their motivations are diverse: some are idealistic, possessed by a need to change the world or serve their brethren; others are in search of money (or power or fame).

Sanjay did not care much for money. In these parts, he had made the leap from being an outsider in society to an insider. Over the past decade, he had gone from being a relatively unknown migrant Sahni young man to 'Sanjay bhaiya' (as sangathan saathis referred to him), the man who fought for the rights of the marginalised.

An insider in society, Sanjay was still very much an outsider in the circles of power. And a much-maligned outsider at that. Nobody in government liked him: the mukhiya and the panchayat secretary detested him, the BDO considered him a menace, the NREGA programme officer called the sangathan useless. Even the subdivisional officer (SDO) had nothing but contempt for Sanjay and his band of mazdoors.

This last fact took me by surprise. The SDO wields considerable power, occupying in the administrative hierarchy a position between a BDO and a district magistrate (DM), the single most important bureaucrat in the district, which is roughly 200 panchayats.

How did the SDO, who sat many rungs above the mukhiyas and the panchayat secretaries, come to have such strong feelings about Sanjay?

In 2017, Chinmaya Kumar, Rajendran Narayanan and I went to meet the SDO under whose jurisdiction Sanjay's village of Ratnauli fell. It was a Saturday, but the SDO had a full work day ahead of her. I cannot remember if it was the day of her darbar, but her room was teeming with anxious petitioners, each with a grievance of their own. Earlier in the morning, we had caught a glimpse of the SDO as she had swept past us in official haste, her footsteps echoing in the subservient stillness that greeted her presence. (As an aside: in government corridors across the country, the powerful provoke the following reactions: bodies stiffen, backs straighten, ears sharpen, heads bow and voices soften with muffled greetings. Through this all, the powerful walk briskly, basking in the glory of all this attention and pretending not to notice.)

Later, in her open court, we got our chance to speak. We spoke to her in the relatively elite tongues of Hindi and English: in this room dominated by the rural poor of Muzaffarpur, neither language was native, but a deferential silence reigned over the fifty or so persons gathered. When we told the SDO that we had spent the previous day in Sanjay's village, her lip curled into a smirk and she asked, 'You met Sanjay Sahni?'

It turned out that she knew him pretty well. The mazdoors of Sanjay's movement, she explained, had even complained to her about ration distributions.

However, she had heard other things about them. She had heard that the mazdoors charge Rs 5,000 from government officials to settle disputes; that Sanjay was a middle-man, a thekedar, someone who blackmailed officials; that he was a public nuisance and did more harm than good. 'While I cannot confirm if it is true,' she said, 'I heard he has even engaged in physical disputes with administrative staff.'

Remarkably for someone who seemed to know so much about the SPSS mazdoors, the SDO had never met Sanjay Sahni, had never been to Ratnauli, and the only woman from SPSS she had met with was Medina Begum, who was the one to file a complaint about rations. The complaint turned out to be genuine and the SDO had resolved the matter. But it had done nothing to change her opinion about Sanjay.

Human civilisation, it is postulated, flourished partly because of its ability to tell stories about the world. The state sustained itself on stories too, spinning yarns not merely about how the government functioned, but also about those who dared question it.

By 2017, Sanjay Sahni had been around for nearly half a dozen years. MNREGA Watch and SPSS had seen their shares of ups and downs: many mazdoors from near and far had joined the movement, and while a large number had remained, some had left and others dithered. Strikes were still organised; battles were fought—for work, ration and pensions—with uneven results; as the years rolled by, roads were built, canals were cleaned, new songs were invented and new technologies, like the smartphone, embraced. SPSS's base ('office' is too formal a term for some of the earlier structures) had moved from Sanjay's home in

Ratnauli to NaREGA Chowk to Ram Babu's house in Mahant Maniyari (and eventually it would move once more to a small plot behind Ram Babu's house). The movement itself had seen a parade of seconds-in-command: Krishna Devi, Reena Devi, Lal Babu, Santhosh Thakur and Mandesar Ram.

Through all this, the local state, jolted out of its routine corrupt ways, had responded fiercely. Mukhiyas across panchayats where the sangathans were active had threatened mazdoors, sometimes going as far as to inflict violence upon them. Others focused on co-opting mazdoors, weaning a few away to cause a break in ranks. BDOs and NREGA programme officers (POs), one step removed from the ground but no less powerful, issued arbitrary orders, and even colluded with bank managers to prevent funds from being withdrawn from mazdoors' bank accounts.

The movement resisted, braving blows and insults, setbacks and defeats.

This caused resentment among the local officials.

And that is when they began to tell tales. Stories about the mazdoors' misdemeanours began doing the rounds, first as gossip, then as fact, and finally as scrupulously fabricated and officially documented claims.

By the summer of 2017, Sanjay Sahni had four FIRs filed against him, on various charges, including punishment for rioting, wrongful restraint, wrongful confinement, assaulting a public official, theft, voluntarily causing grievous hurt, criminal intimidation and attempt to murder.

Sanjay Sahni, electrician and activist, had added one more descriptor to his identity: alleged criminal.

Here is the story of one accusation against Sanjay and the mazdoors, told through the lens of the state. To understand this tale better, one must acquaint oneself with the principal cast of government actors responsible for implementing the NREGA. Below, I present the two of them, in descending order of importance (and, consequently, ascending order of corruption):

The block programme officer: The PO is the authority on whose shoulders the final burden of implementing the NREGA in the entire block rests. Jeetendra Kumar, the PO of Kurhani, Sanjay's block, is an animated and colourful character, someone we will encounter later in this chapter. The PO lords over thirty-nine gram panchayats.

The panchayat rozgar sevak: The PRS, alongside the mukhiya, is one of the two main players responsible for implementing the NREGA in panchayats. The PRS, unlike the mukhiya, is not elected, but appointed by the local state. Shambhunath Singh, the PRS of Ratnauli does not live in the village, but travels to and fro every few days to monitor NREGA activities in the village.

Arguably the mukhiya is the most important actor in implementing the NREGA. However, the mukhiya of Ratnauli was disengaged from an active part in the NREGA. The mazdoors' vigilance meant he had no real route to make money off the scheme. Inevitably, over time, he lost interest and let the mazdoors run the programme in the panchayat.

Now, to return to the tale, told from the perspective of the local state.

On the last day of March in 2017, PRS Shambhunath Singh arrived at an NREGA worksite in Ratnauli. At the worksite, Singh counted a total of 153 labourers working on creating pokhars–tanks to collect water for irrigation. He went on to collect signatures (or, in this instance, mostly thumb prints) of workers present on the attendance sheet, a 'muster roll'.

He soon discovered a fact that troubled him: some of the mazdoors' names were not on the muster rolls.

A little after noon, Sanjay showed up. He began instigating the mazdoors whose names were absent from the muster roll to sign on the sheet. Singh protested. How could people whose names were not on the attendance sheet sign? The mazdoors were in no mood to listen. They grew raucous, the situation heated, the mid-afternoon sun blazed away. It was Singh against 153 workers and Sanjay Sahni. Suddenly, five mazdoors—including the small and grey-haired Mandesri Devi—snatched the muster roll from Singh's hands and tore it, the pieces showering down like confetti upon a cheering crowd.

Singh panicked. He decided to flee the scene, but the mazdoors, now sensing blood, pounced on him. With Sanjay leading them, they beat him up. Singh, whose chest bore wounds, somehow managed to call his superior—the PO for Kurhani Block. Jeetendra Kumar, the PO, arrived on the scene immediately. He bravely fought off the mazdoors and rescued Singh. They went straight to the Sadar Hospital in Muzaffarpur to treat Singh's wounds.

That night, still in hospital, Singh and the PO filed an FIR. Sanjay Sahni and the mazdoors were accused of violating Sections 147, 149, 341, 342, 353, 379, 504 and 506 of the Indian Penal Code.

Singh's story above—rich in detail and superbly captured in the FIR—would have had a semblance of credibility had it not been for this one fact: on 31 March 2017, Sanjay Sahni, the main accused, was 384 kilometres away from the scene of the crime, visiting his family in Ranchi. He had taken a bus on 29 March (the ticket of which he had faithfully retained) from Muzaffarpur to Ranchi. Besides, on the day of the alleged incident, he had met with Jean Drèze in Ranchi.[102]

What then happened on 31 March 2017 at the NREGA worksite?

Kishun Sahni, ward member, Ward No. 5, Ratnauli Panchayat, was among those present on the day of the incident. Kishun, like the other ward members we have seen before, was part-mazdoor, part-local government official.

On the morning of 31 March, somebody in the village had alerted him to the fact that PRS Shambhunath Singh had come to the panchayat and was apparently visiting the NREGA worksite. Kishun hastened to make it to the worksite. He wanted to meet with the PRS and discuss with him the prospect of starting a new NREGA project in the upcoming weeks. In addition, he wanted to make sure his attendance was marked, for he had also worked on the worksite Singh was inspecting.

When Kishun Sahni arrived at the worksite, he noticed the PRS and mazdoors in the midst of a heated argument. One mazdoor, Siri Sahni, was requesting the PRS to let him sign on the muster roll: 'I have been waiting for a long time to sign.' The PRS abused him and said he was not Siri Sahni's baap ka naukar, the servant of his father. An angry Siri responded that the PRS was still a sarkari naukar, a servant of the government.

Indu Devi, a long-time SPSS supporter, and some other women intervened. They stood between the two men—thereby preventing them from coming to blows—and tried to reason

---

[102] In Ranchi, Sanjay had also visited an ATM and his bank, updated his passbook and withdrawn money. He kept records of all these activities.

with the PRS. They spoke to him calmly, telling him to leave. The PRS, beside himself with rage, lunged towards Siri Sahni, striking Indu Devi squarely in the stomach. Though hurt, Indu Devi did not back down. Instead, calm as still water, she said: '*Bhaiya! Chhod dijiye na. Aap kaam kar rahe hain, kaam kijiye, jhanjhat nahin kijiye.*' (Brother! Let it be. Please do your job and don't pick a fight.)

The PRS was in no mood to reason. Angry at being separated from Siri, he turned his anger towards the women: 'I will take you all away from your house.'

There was some more shouting, following which the PRS had had enough: in a huff, he collected all the muster rolls, got on his motorcycle and sped away.

Kishun Sahni still wanted to speak with the PRS, so he followed him on his bicycle. A few minutes later, he spotted the PRS, the PO and a few others standing around their parked motorcycles. The PO had come all the way from Kurhani town. From a distance, Kishun saw that the PO and the PRS were speaking animatedly. By the time he approached them, they had stopped talking. The PO then tore off the PRS's shirt and carefully applied some mud on it. He then took a few steps backwards, pulled out his phone and snapped a picture of the PRS in that dishevelled state and sent it to higher government officials, namely the BDO and the district development commissioner (DDC).

The PO and the PRS then planned their next steps: they decided to proceed to Muzaffarpur town, get the PRS admitted in a hospital and file an FIR. Seeing Kishun there, the PO, who saw him as a junior confrère–a man who was on the 'inside'–invited him to join them in their Muzaffarpur antics.

Kishun, neither insider or outsider, refused: his loyalties lay with the truth.

The seven motorcycles sped away, leaving a cloud of dust in their wake.

That night, Shambhunath Singh was admitted in Sadar Hospital, Muzaffarpur. An attendant at the hospital, who was on duty when Singh was admitted, remembered the night well when interviewed a few weeks later. He said:[103]

> I remember it was a Friday night. The PRS was perfectly fine. He had nothing [no issues] but was admitted in the hospital on a whim. [He] came ... with a lot of people on motorbikes ... There was no space to move around. The entire hospital was crowded [with] what seemed like the entire district staff of NREGA. All [the PRS] had was just mud on his body and nothing else. The PRS said that he was hurt but I couldn't find anything wrong with him but if a patient comes and says that he is hurt, then we have to give some medication ... He was perfectly fine. He was just acting like he was hurt.

The next morning, Kishun Sahni woke up to read in the papers that the workers of Ratnauli had torn off the shirt of the hapless PRS and created a ruckus.

The reason we can piece together such a detailed narrative of events for 31 March 2017 is Rajendran Narayanan's meticulous fact-finding report. He led a team that investigated the four FIRs against Sanjay Sahni. Coincidentally, I was in Ratnauli around the time Rajendran was conducting his final set of interviews. He invited me to tag along, and so, one blazing

[103] Rajendran Narayanan, *Fact Finding Report: Slew of FIRs against Sanjay Sahni in Muzaffarpur, Bihar*, 2017. See: https://archive.azimpremjiuniversity.edu.in/SitePages/pdf/SanjaySahniFactFindingReportJune2017.pdf.

summer morning in 2017, Chinmaya, Rajendran and I paid a visit to Jeetendra Kumar, the NREGA programme officer who had, as per Kishun Sahni, orchestrated the FIR.

Jeetendra Kumar came with a reputation. The mazdoors of the sangathans considered him a scourge. On the other hand, the local grievance redressal officer, Manoj Kumar, thought him to be quite 'dynamic'. This opinion was shared by many members on the inside–the mukhiyas, the BDO, the SDO–who celebrated him as a model officer.

Kumar was an interesting study: he looked like an intellectual, sporting spectacles and a premature salt-and-pepper beard; a hairline that had retreated to the back of his oval head served to indicate a precocious wisdom; he dressed like an educated everyman: a collared shirt, a pen in his pocket, formal pants. He spoke with a sense of feisty urgency, rarely stealing a breath between words. Oddly, he always seemed to be making pronouncements to a larger audience, though there were only the four of us in that room.

At the very outset–and several times afterwards–Kumar boasted about his achievements as an NREGA PO: he was, he reminded us repeatedly, a multiple-year nominee to the list of top five NREGA POs in the state. Under the Act, he had created assets worth crores of rupees, planted thousands of trees and had generated a stupendous 3,49,000 person days of work. He painted himself as an NREGA messiah, tirelessly bestowing work and wages on the weak and often unworthy.

He had other skills too: in a previous posting as PO in Raxaul district of West Champaran, Jitendra Kumar had successfully put out an activist's flame by threatening to file an FIR against him. Now, transferred to Kurhani, he had gone about single-mindedly helping the poor. He boasted about how the panchayats of Ratnauli, Mahant Maniyari and Amrak had seen payments worth over a crore of rupees, with zero corruption to boot. We were surprised, because these panchayats were sangathan-strongholds and had long served as a thorn in the flesh of the state.

When we asked about the role of the mazdoor sangathan in these panchayats, Kumar said: 'What is the point of having civil society groups where the system is already in good shape?' It was an absurd claim: the sangathans in those panchayats—SPSS and MW—were responsible for rooting out the corruption in the first place. It was akin to asking what use for an engine in a car that seems to be moving quite well on its own.

But these claims were merely appetizers. The entrée was Trumpian in its relationship to the truth. Corruption in the NREGA, Kumar declared, owed its basis not to the mukhiyas or the BDO or others like him in government, but to the mazdoors and their laziness. He declaimed to the room at large: 'The day a mazdoor starts working well, there will be no corruption.' The chief culprits, he continued, were women and old people, for they slowed down the work and contributed to delays. This necessitated the use of machines, an excess of which was banned under the NREGA. Records, therefore, had to be fudged to cover for the ineptitude of the old and the infirm.

This was a preposterous claim on many grounds: first, payments for NREGA work were often made conditional on the amount of work done: measurements of the total amount of work done were carefully made by engineers and then payments were decided. If someone worked less, they got paid less too. Second, in the panchayats he was referring to, the older women (the Mandesri Devis and the Chandrakala Devis) were among the hardest workers anywhere. Third, his hypothesis flew in the face of conventional wisdom—bolstered by years' worth of well-documented research and activism—on corruption in the

NREGA, which pointed fingers (all ten of them) at the state. If corruption was caused by laziness on the part of the mazdoors, then why would transparency-promoting measures like digitised payment systems or smart-cards *increase* the wages they received? If they were truly lazy, these transparency measures would only serve to show them up in a poor light and reduce their wages.

For dessert, Kumar served up a delicious rant on 'social audits'. Since it was impossible to eliminate lazy persons from the scheme, Kumar said he would personally run social audits to keep tabs on corruption. He would, he said, create an agency of 'well-meaning, literate persons' who would go around villages squaring official data with workers'—and local officials'—testimonies.

It was clear as day that Kumar had barely given any thought to social audits. Had he done so, he would have realised that the NREGA already had a provision for audits; that auditors travelled to villages and collected testimonies from workers; that, for such audits to work, implementing officers such as himself would have to keep away; that audits work best bottom-up, when they place citizens' voices at the centre, and not that of individuals considered to be 'well-meaning' or the elite who were hand-picked by the administration.

As the interview wore on, it became clear that Jeetendra Kumar was chiefly responsible for the multiple FIRs against Sanjay Sahni and the mazdoors. He had, by his own admission, honed this fake-FIR-fuelled intimidation strategy at a previous posting and was now using the sangathans of Kurhani as a finishing school for perfecting his methods. Was he—and here I am merely speculating—transferred to Kurhani because of his previous successes at quelling civil society groups?

When asked what had happened on 31 March 2017, Kumar, speaking even more forcefully than he had all afternoon—

perhaps to completely drown out the feeble protesting whispers of his conscience—said:[104]

> It was the last day of work on a farm pond. The PRS frequently takes attendance and at around 3:30 PM on the 31st of March, 2017, the PRS called me and told me that there was some altercation with him at the work site. As such an FIR was filed. The labourers should salute the PRS for the work done but his shirt was torn by the workers. I didn't go to the place but the PRS sent me a photo of him with a lot of mud and a torn shirt. I don't remember who the FIR was filed against. I am guessing Sanjay Sahni's name was there in the FIR. So I feel that Sanjay Sahni is a repeated offender. The PRS was in Sadar Hospital for 3 days between 31st March and 2nd April.

At some point during this meal of a monologue, a man burst into the room. Standing at the door and staring straight at us, he barked: 'Are you all representing the mazdoors of SPSS or are you on the side of the panchayat rozgar sevak?' Kumar did not give us a chance to respond and asked the man to leave.

The train of Kumar's words halted briefly when we asked him who the man was, but it picked up steam soon enough and jumped tracks entirely, leaving our query hanging.

By the time I got to witness Sanjay Sahni make his 'man on the inside' campaign pitch to mazdoors in the summer of 2019, the FIR tally had risen. There were now six.

---

104 Rajendran Narayanan, *Fact Finding Report: Slew of FIRs against Sanjay Sahni in Muzaffarpur, Bihar*, 2017. See: https://archive.azimpremjiuniversity.edu.in/SitePages/pdf/SanjaySahniFactFindingReportJune2017.pdf.

The tales ranged from the far-fetched to the absurd. Consider this, for instance: Shivlal Shah of Balra Kishun village committed suicide while his wife was away working on an NREGA worksite. An FIR was filed against Mandesri Devi and Sanjay Sahni for persuading '*the wife of the deceased to accompany them in connection with some work under* MANREGA'. Apparently, Shivlal Yadav did not want his wife to go and hence committed suicide. The court order from the bail hearing noted: 'the deceased was protesting against the decision of his wife, Neelam Devi, to go with them and since, despite his protest, his wife accompanied the accused persons, he committed suicide'. And so, Mandesri Devi—who exudes the warmth of a favourite grandmother—was accused of culpable homicide amounting to murder.

The most enterprising accusation of all featured a Tarantino-esque revenge-of-the-oppressed fantasy. Here is a slightly dramatised recounting of facts from the victim's—the PRS of Amrak—perspective. He, like any dutiful government servant, was at an NREGA worksite making sure work was progressing smoothly when, all of a sudden, Sanjay Sahni, who was not a resident of Amrak, and a group of seven or eight angry mazdoors showed up at the scene. Led by Sahni, these mazdoors pounced on the hapless PRS and thrashed him. Not yet satisfied, they conjured a Bolero—a vehicle, one must note, that is worth lakhs of rupees. To rent one for even a day would cost a small fortune, something the mazdoors can ill afford. Yet, there they were, Bolero at hand and a cowering PRS at their feet. Sanjay then took the wheels of the Bolero, and pitilessly drove it straight *over* the PRS's leg. The other mazdoors gleefully watched, and cheered, at this shining example of bloodlust. Finally, they made away with a bundle of muster rolls the PRS was carrying.

The state knew these claims would not hold in court. Yet, they filed FIR upon FIR, in a country where such a filing would take the average person weeks of perseverance or a call from someone powerful. The FIRs made life hard for Sanjay and the mazdoors. They found a lawyer, made regular trips to the local court. This was expensive, both money- and time-wise: workdays were missed, meals were sacrificed. This precarious existence was compounded by a constant fear: one decision against them may mean time in jail.

In life, as in sport, one's judgement wilts under sustained pressure. Sanjay saw the assembly line of FIRs for what it was: a systematic attempt by the local state to quash the movement. But also, at times, he mistook it for what it was not: a conspiracy against him by the most powerful men in Patna. On more than one occasion, Sanjay told me how the mukhiya of Ratnauli—a JD(U) man—was backed by Chief Minister Nitish Kumar. This was unlikely: mukhiyas, important as they may be, number over 8,400, far too many for the chief minister of Bihar to take a personal interest in. Yet, in 2016, Sanjay dashed off a letter to the CM alleging all sorts of corruption and calling out the district magistrate by name. This letter was duly forwarded to the district administration, which only further served to alienate the mazdoors from the local state.

A few months later, Sanjay and a group of mazdoors organised a rail roko. This is a form of resistance where protestors occupy railroad tracks and stop trains from moving. They were protesting yet another scuffle featuring a mazdoor being pushed by a PRS. The response of the mazdoors—to stop the movement of trains, thereby inconveniencing scores of ordinary men and women—seemed incommensurate with the provocation.

On one occasion, at a joint meeting featuring a team of

mazdoors and a group of bureaucrats, Sanjay and the mazdoors were suspicious of a phone call that a senior bureaucrat received in the middle of the meeting. They assumed the call was from someone high-up in Patna, and they convinced themselves that it caused the bureaucrat to change his stance, from being initially sympathetic towards their cause to turning against them. Chinmaya and I, who were both present at the meeting, knew this to not be the case. In this instance, the bureaucrat's behaviour merely reflected the evidence he was being presented with by members of the local state, who had turned up for the meeting better prepared. It was just one of those rare occasions where the local state's story was somewhat credible. The phone call was irrelevant.

I do not recount these examples to excuse the excesses of the local state. The fantasies of the local state had real consequences: its fictitious accusations against the mazdoors endangered people's lives and livelihoods. In contrast, the conspiracy theories of the mazdoors were harmless, never really sticking. If anything, with every accusation the mazdoors threw at them, the local officers' reputations only seemed to grow in the eyes of those who mattered.

We go about our lives telling ourselves—and others—a story about who we are. Not always is that story going to align fully with the truth. The truth is messy, complex and chaotic. The stories are linear and comforting. They have beginnings and ends, they make sense, they keep us going.

Now, imagine if you were up against the whole world; imagine you were pushed into a corner, pulverised from all sides. The stories then acquire a new purpose. They do not merely fulfil our need for order in our lives. They give us something more.

The stories of our oppression now provide ballast.

Every story becomes a call to action. Yet, embedded within each such tale, there is also a story full of beauty: it is one brimming with hope.

You act because you dream.

And you dream of a story where the scheming mighty fall because the many weak fight as one unbroken whole.

Muzaffarpur, June 2019

After lunch, which is the aforementioned egg curry (that makes your mouth water twice: first in anticipation and then again when you eat it, thanks to its tongue-scorching spiciness), I enter the office to see Kanti Devi still eating. She is among the tallest women in these parts; she has a pleasing face and a nose-ring that accentuates her sharp features. We make small talk. She tells me that Sanjay is yet to travel to her village, which is only a few kilometres away. I tell her we will have to rectify that. After all, Sanjay's election campaign–whose shy beginnings we had jointly witnessed that morning–has to first go where he has most support. And Kanti Devi and the women in her village are among the most passionate SPSS/MW supporters going around.

'Do you think he will win?' I ask her in Hindi.

'Of course!' she says. 'We are all with him!'

I am not surprised. A deluge of hope powers the electric activism of the mazdoors. I prod further. The task ahead is enormous, I tell her. Cruelly, like an elder explaining death to a child, I break down the numbers for her.

There are thirty-nine panchayats in Kurhani. Perhaps, the sangathan has 100 members in each? No, 200—she corrects me. Okay, that's about 8,000 mazdoors. Let's round upwards to about 10,000. Let's say they ALL vote for Sanjay. Will that be enough?

She's not sure.

I tell her it's about 1/6th the way there.

But the sangathan's mazdoors, she says, are not alone. Each one of them has a family. The whole family will vote.

Even then, assuming there are two additional votes per household, we will have about 30,000 votes for Sanjay. That is the best-case scenario. We need at least double that number.

Where will we get these votes from?

As the question hangs in the air, her face goes through a gamut of emotions: first, acknowledgement; then surprise, which gives way to fear almost immediately. I can see the scene in my mind as I type: the dark, windowless office room; the dampness of the mud floor on my bare feet; and Kanti Devi, the weight of the task at hand finally upon her and visible in every pore of her face, which has now morphed into an expression of dull nothingness.

Have I gone too far?

Should I not have said what I did?

And then, just as suddenly as the fear gripped her face, it is gone. She's back. Her face arranges itself into a smile and she says:

'We still have a year. We will campaign everywhere. *Hum jeetenge*. We will win!'

It is a lovely story, a beautiful delusion.

All progress, Bernard Shaw once said, depends on the unreasonable man.

On that afternoon in Ratnauli, it seemed to depend on a collective of unreasonable women.

8

An Inextinguishable Flame

Late one night in Washington DC, I received this message on WhatsApp from Sanjay:

> *Ratnauli hero is now go to man for maigrets*
> *Saran g iska hindi kya hoga, plz bataiyega.*

The message contained a link to an article in the Delhi-based magazine *Civil Society*. The article applauded Sanjay's tireless efforts towards the cause of migrant workers caught in 'the gales of the coronavirus storm'.[105] Someone had forwarded the article to Sanjay, but even the English-language headline was beyond his comprehension. Hence, he had sent it to me.

Sanjay's message was rooted in a world that easily straddled many conflicting forces–the old and the new, rural and urban, Hindi and English. He had misspelt 'migrants' as (the rather avian-sounding) 'maigrets'; he had used the spelling that would be preferred by most Biharis for my name: 'Saran'. In Bihar,

105 Report of 29 June 2020: Civil Society News, 'Ratnauli hero is now go-to man for migrants', *Civil Society*, https://www.civilsocietyonline.com/campaigns/ratnauli-hero-now-migrants-go-to-man-in-bihar/.

Sh was always S.[106] He had added the traditional honorific 'ji' to my name, but spelt it with the snazzy single-letter G. It was a message in Hindi, but typed out in Roman alphabet. There was one English word in his message, though: the word 'please', which he spelt, as any cool twenty-first-century person would, as 'plz'.

Translated to English, his message said: 'Ratnauli hero is now go-to man for migrants. Sharan-ji, what would this be in Hindi, please tell?'

A full year had passed since I travelled to Ratnauli to watch Sanjay Sahni and the mazdoors dream about a neta on the inside. I had since returned to the US and was now ensconced in an apartment in DC as a pandemic raged outside. The novel coronavirus had wrecked my travel plans to India and Bihar that summer. In addition, owing to arbitrary visa regulations, I was resigned to the fact that I would play no physical part in Sanjay's election campaign. My role would be as a source of remote assistance, acting as a campaign sounding-board, helping with fund-raising, rounding up volunteers and building social-media teams.

And occasionally, as in the case of the text message, doubling up as a translator.

From April to early November of 2020, Sanjay's campaign took over increasingly large chunks of my life. Yet, looking back as I write this in February 2021, I feel very little emotion. There are two reasons for this: first, *distance*. The countless phone conversations and debates with Sanjay and his supporters, the vivid accounts of the campaign by friends and volunteers,

---

[106] Abhishek was Abhisek; and a correction was a correcsun. In the larger scheme of things, these 'mistakes' didn't matter one bit: there was no gap in communication.

the scores of photos and videos of brave women and belligerent men cannot substitute for the smell of burnt chai at the chaiwallah's at Salais Sthan or the faint whiff of marijuana from Somariya Devi's hookah. This absence of visceral engagement was compounded by a sense of guilt. '*Kab aaoge aap?*' Sanjay would ask, and add in a mocking tone, '*Agle saal?*' (When will you come [and help with the campaign]? Next year? [After the elections?])

A second reason for my detachedness was the result. Sanjay's campaign was doomed from the start: mazdoors, however popular, do not contest elections, let alone win them. Yet, a part of me hoped. Not for victory, but for a contest.

That was not to be.

This chapter, therefore, plays out partly as narrative-from-a-distance and partly as an excavation, a rummaging among debris of a blanked-out annihilation.

By late 2019, Sanjay and the mazdoors had begun preparing for their campaign in earnest. Mazdoor supporters from across the constituency of Kurhani—and in SPSS/MW strongholds from neighbouring areas—had been told Sanjay would contest the upcoming MLA elections. He then made a few day trips to villages in his constituency of Kurhani on the SPSS tempo (a large auto-rickshaw, locally called 'taympu') and met with supporters. He was welcomed with much fanfare: images from early January 2020 show Sanjay, his palms folded, surrounded by a crowd of (mostly) women mazdoors, his head peering from above a preponderance of marigold maalas that seemed to have colonised his neck, shoulders and torso.

By February, some online campaigning had begun in the form of WhatsApp posters that were being circulated among core supporters. One poster featured two faces against a blue background: the first belonged to Kedar Gupta, the incumbent BJP MLA; the second, Sanjay Sahni. The caption below the image read: '*Bihar main BJP ke iss dabang vidhayak ko iss baar chunaav main takkar dega ye mazdoor.*' (This strongman BJP MLA from Bihar will be challenged by this mazdoor.) Another WhatsApp poster showed Sanjay amidst a sea of mazdoors, his fists clenched and raised. This was captioned (in Hindi): *This boy will make the BJP lose their deposit and his name is Sanjay Sahni.*

Later in February, with six months to go for election day, Sanjay called me and asked to help raise some funds for a 'Mahapanchayat' the mazdoors wanted to organise. The idea was to orchestrate a grand gathering of mazdoors in Mahant Maniyari, where SPSS/MW was headquartered, and announce Sanjay as the candidate for the upcoming elections. Sanjay hoped to invite the economist Jean Drèze and the activists Aruna Roy and Nikhil Dey.

A poster was printed and circulated asking mazdoors to come to Mahant Maniyari: '*Maniyari Chalein, Maniyari Chalein, Maniyari Chalein.*' (Let's go to Maniyari!) The poster had prominently advertised the date of the Mahapanchayat—29 March—when, it claimed, the mazdoors would announce their Lok Ummeedvar, People's Candidate. At the bottom, in quotes, was a cheeky sales line: *Aana na bhooliye.* (Don't forget to come.)

'Will you come to the Mahapanchayat?' Sanjay asked me over the phone. I was then in India, having made a short trip in late February. I explained to Sanjay that I could not make it, for I had tickets to return to the US on 16 March. I had a PhD to complete and a graduation to attend. But, I told him, I would be back in the summer and would immerse myself in the campaign.

Neither the Mahapanchayat nor the graduation nor my return to India came to be.

These events—important as they seemed at the time—were insignificant rafts swept away by the gales of the COVID-19 storm.

In the early weeks of the pandemic, as workers from across India scrambled to get back to their villages, Sanjay Sahni served as an oasis of hope for scores of deserted migrants. Flying blind in the face of an invisible enemy, the Government of India, amidst clanging vessels and motivational speeches, announced a nationwide lockdown with only four hours' notice.[107] Everything was closed: businesses, educational institutions, government offices. While the city-based haves learnt to wash their own vessels, those without the means carried a lifetime's belongings—mattresses, clothes, jewellery—and traversed hundreds of kilometres back to their villages, their scuffling feet punctuating the silence of the motorless highways.

The plight of the migrants hit close to home in more than one way for Sanjay. He was no stranger to the precarious existence of migrant workers, having been one himself for years. Moreover, his village of Ratnauli had seen hundreds of returning migrants. Moved by their plight, but even more so by a sense of justice, Sanjay plunged into relief work.

There were three categories of migrants: first, those who wanted to return to the villages, but could not risk walking; second, those who were looking to stay on in the cities, but did not have the resources to do so; third, those who had found a way back to their villages, but were now rendered helpless.

---

107 Jeffrey Gettleman and Kai Schultz, 'Modi Orders 3-Week Total Lockdown for All 1.3 Billion Indians', *The New York Times*, 24 March 2020, https://www.nytimes.com/2020/03/24/world/asia/india-coronavirus-lockdown.html.

All three types of migrants reached out to Sanjay, who was besieged with calls. The *Civil Society* report he had alerted me to said:

> Sahni empathizes with the callers. He also tries to help them through the new maze they find themselves in. And from one to the next his number has been passed around so many times that the calls don't stop.

Sanjay was uniquely positioned to help the third type of migrant—those who had returned to their villages, but were unable to find work or access state benefits. He had spent a decade organising work for mazdoors under the NREGA. Sanjay knew the ration, pension and cash-benefits systems like the back of his hand. He patiently explained the nitty-gritties of the NREGA law, encouraging mazdoors to demand work, using the internet to check if their job cards were intact or, in other cases, checking for active worksites in their villages for them.

The lion's share of the calls Sanjay received were from those in the cities. These persons, mostly employed in India's vast informal sector as construction workers, shop assistants, factory labour, watchmen, had seen the overnight closure of their worksites. The thekedars, contractors, who had brought them to these distant lands had disappeared, their phones unreachable. The local ration dealers had stopped supplying grains on loan.

In fact, the very first distress call Sanjay received was from a resident of Ratnauli who was now stuck in far-off Karnataka. The migrant and his family had neither money nor food. Sanjay and the mazdoors from Ratnauli pooled together Rs 6,000 and transferred it to the migrant family's bank account. Word soon went around that a group of mazdoors led by Sanjay, sitting in Ratnauli, were offering help.

Sanjay played information diffuser, keeping migrant families abreast of the new schemes that governments had launched for them. He also spent hours teaching mazdoors how to access these benefits.[108] Sometimes he played matchmaker, linking families who were in the same city with each other, so they could pool resources and hold on in the city or travel back to the villages together.

The remote nature of assistance played directly into Sanjay's strengths as an activist. He had always been a very twenty-first-century mobiliser, relying overwhelmingly on technology to channel struggles and build bridges. Not for him the old model of travelling village to village and making fiery speeches. Instead, he preferred his trusted phone and the internet to seek out and be sought out by mazdoors.[109] Thus, when the pandemic hit, Sanjay, cooped up in his tiny office in Ratnauli, did what he knew best: work the phones.

He was instrumental in conceptualising the Stranded Workers' Action Network (SWAN), a nationwide volunteer-driven effort to provide information, resources and institutional support for stranded migrant workers. Within a month, SWAN had attended to calls from over 16,000 workers.[110] By October,

---

108 The Bihar government had stipulated that migrant workers be sent Rs 1,000 to their bank accounts. To be eligible, a migrant had to prove their status as a migrant and have their bank account and Aadhaar number registered with the government. In practice, this amounted to negotiating a set of tiresome rules and considerable red tape. Sanjay had, of course, made a career out of snipping red tape. And so, he fielded calls from panicky migrants, desperate for some relief, teaching them the tricks he'd picked up: websites one could access, people you could call, forms to be filled, photocopies to be done and so on.

109 Over the years, my Ratnauli-itineraries have come to include some time carved out for local travel. On these trips, I look forward to the delight on the face of the mazdoors—some of whom would have worked with Sanjay for years—as they introduce their villages and their homes to Sanjay.

110 A May 2020 report by SWAN: https://covid19socialsecurity.files.wordpress.com/2020/05/32-days-and-counting_swan.pdf.

SWAN had assisted more than 36,000 workers.[111]

In all this, the novel coronavirus, the root cause of all these troubles, remained invisible and forgotten. In May, I asked Sanjay if people were catching the virus and falling ill in his parts. He said he really could not tell if there was a rise in illnesses or deaths. People were far more worried, he told me, about the lockdown and consequent restrictions.

As for deaths, he had this to report:

'*Log pehle bhi marte thhe, abhi bhi mar rahe hain.*' (People have always been dying and they die now too.)

Sanjay's election campaign, still motoring on the runway when the pandemic hit, did not take off till months later. It was only in June—when India launched 'Unlock 1.0' after four phases of crippling lockdowns—that he and the mazdoors began to pick up the strands of the campaign.

The first posters were printed, celebrating Sanjay as the chosen ummeedwaar of the mazdoors. The poster had printed slogans in blue, but 'Sanjay Sahni' was displayed in bold red font. A picture of Sanjay took up one half of the poster: clean-shaven, cheeks full, oiled hair neatly combed to a side, clad in a blue-and-white chequered shirt, a blue tee-shirt peeking from beneath his neckline. The contrast between this picture and a photograph from a 2012 piece in the *Civil Society* magazine—

111 One of SWAN's key organisers wrote: 'It was persistent requests from Sanjay that prompted the setting up of SWAN. He then acted as the nodal point between thousands of stranded migrant workers and the SWAN volunteers. Despite being neck deep in distress calls during this period, Sanjay would patiently assess the needs of every caller and coordinate with SWAN volunteers in ensuring that relief reached those in distress. Thousands of workers across the country benefited from his relentless efforts.'

taken around the time I had first met him—was stark: there, Sanjay's face was gaunt and angular, his hair somewhat shabbier, his cheeks unshaven, a plain white shirt drooping over his skinny shoulders, a pen tucked into his pocket. As I stared at Sanjay's face in the poster, I remember thinking that he had come a long way. In neither photograph did he resemble a typical neta.[112] But while he looked like an activist in the former (framed as he was with women mazdoors in the backdrop), he exuded a more conventional sense of power in the latter.

By late June, teams of women mazdoors, armed with large bottles of glue, were travelling around Kurhani and pasting posters. They chose prominent public display points—the high school compound wall, the panchayat building, chai shops, ration shops, a lamp post at the weekly haat (market), atop a tall tree. Many proudly displayed the posters on the outer walls of their homes. Teams also went house-to-house distributing pamphlets. This involved travelling fairly long distances on foot, wearing masks made out of dupattas or pieces of old clothing. Sanjay told me that teams of men, then youth and finally the old were next in line to build on the work of the women.

---

[112] For years, I had seen Sanjay struggle with the term 'neta'. When someone would describe him thus, perhaps at the chai shop or in casual conversation with him, he would wince and correct them. 'I am not a neta, just a social worker.' He didn't want to be seen as 'one of them', as someone who had sullied himself by indulging in the dirty world of politics. I remember once gently ribbing Sanjay about what I thought were his neta-like mannerisms. While walking on the streets of Ratnauli, he would acknowledge the presence of passers-by by bringing his arm to his chest and saying: '*Theek hai, theek hai.*' (Fine, fine.) It was a polite, somewhat perfunctory gesture, and not uncommon. It was the frequency with which he did it that astounded me. He seemed to know everyone who walked past him, rich or poor, man or woman. I remember joking with him that this was a sure sign that he may be turning into a people's person, perhaps even a neta himself. He laughed. I have never seen him make that gesture since.

All this did not imply that the migrant relief work was over for Sanjay. As he told me over WhatsApp in early June: '*Din men pravasi mazdoor ko madad karna padta hai aur rat men election ki tyari.*' (I have to help migrant workers during the day and prepare for elections in the night.)

July saw no decline in the number of COVID-19 cases in India. Yet, many cities and villages across the country had opened up, beginning their long journey back to normalcy.

Muzaffarpur, though, had to wait.

Flooding is an annual affair in these parts—like the Chhat Pooja that succeeds Diwali or encephalitis during the lychee season. This time, however, the situation was particularly bad: for days on end, dark clouds loomed over the landscape, sending persistent showers. The water rose in stages: first, the rivers and canals cannibalised their banks, then the fields became waterlogged, then the unfinished drains were flooding, then the pathways between homes became unusable, and finally, the roads too were engulfed. Before long, aerial shots of villages showed islands of human settlements in a world of beige-brown water, connected only by electric poles strung together like the first foundations of a bridge.

Campaigning was put on pause once more. The mazdoors turned to organising help for those affected. On 22 July, Sanjay wrote a letter to the DM asking for the immediate release of relief materials for all flood-affected villages in the sixteen blocks of Muzaffarpur. Otherwise, the mazdoors threatened to go on strike. Sanjay and MW circulated an appeal among their well-wishers—who were mostly activists and supporters from outside Bihar—asking for funds. People duly responded.

However, and incredibly, an equally large share of funds came from the mazdoors themselves: many dug into their meagre savings, cobbling together resources for those worse off than themselves.

The most affected villages were, in fact, not in Kurhani, the constituency Sanjay was contesting from. Yet, the MW mazdoors carried money and food and travelled–by foot or on bicycles–to Mushahari and Gaighat, the worst affected blocks, to help those who had lost their homes and livelihoods. The MW women walked in water that came up to their chests. On their heads, they carried cloth bundles filled with rations and cash, which they distributed to those huddled in small patches of dry islands amidst flowing waters.

These acts exemplified the spirit of collectiveness that characterised MW's workers. The prominent Hindi daily, *Dainik Jagran*, in a glowing piece about the MW women's activities, said:[113]

> Women working in MNREGA come from extremely poor families. These households have neither land nor other [significant] sources of income. Yet, in these times, they have collected money and have helped nearly 20,000 families affected by floods.

By Independence Day, campaigning had resumed. The winds and the rains had receded, taking with them all the old posters and hoardings the women mazdoors had painstakingly put up.

---

113 Muraru Kumar, 'Misaal Kaayam Kar Rahe Manrega Mazdoor, Baadh Prabhaviton Ke Beech Baant Rahe Raahat Samagri', *Jagran*, 11 August 2020, https://jagran.com/bihar/muzaffarpur-mnrega-laborers-distributing-relief-materials-among-flood-affected-people-in-muzaffarpur-20615308.html.

So, once more, teams of volunteers—this time, mostly young men—set out under cloudy skies, travelling often by foot, but also piling atop one another on tempos or squeezing four to a motorcycle. An image from late August shows one man sitting on another's shoulder and pasting a poster on a tall tree bark. Another shows a clutch of smiling women holding a five-foot-long flex banner that was fluttering in the late-monsoon wind and posing for the camera.

Things moved rapidly over the next few weeks. A team comprising Sanjay, a dozen mazdoors, a tempo, a loudspeaker and a mic, began doing the rounds of villages. With the help of local mazdoors who were affiliated with MW/SPSS, they set up roadside election rallies in these villages. These mazdoors would identify clearings that served as makeshift campaign sites: sometimes a stretch on the edge of verdant fields, other times a patch of fallow land between houses or even a derelict shed by the main market. They would then lay out brightly coloured tarpaulin and gather a small crowd.

Sanjay and his team would soon arrive. This would attract some more people. A couple of 'hellos' and 'mic cheayks' on their rudimentary sound system would cause brief hushes. Some more curious onlookers, fancying a mid-day piece of entertainment, would make their way to join the crowd.

And soon, they would begin. Usually, a few mazdoors would sing a song or two. The songs would speak of injustice and hope, but also emphasise Sanjay's heroics. As with all their songs, the fiery lyrics would be drowned out by the funereal tune and a collective delivery that only a very sympathetic reviewer could term poignant.

Songs done, the atmosphere would turn sombre. Sanjay—mic in one hand, kerchief in another—would take centrestage. He would speak extempore, but his speeches traversed familiar paths, covering truths realised over a decade and distilled into powerful lines. He would tell them his story, beginning with his humble beginnings and his life as a migrant worker, a pravaasi mazdoor. The post-corona world had brought those two words—migrant and worker—into sharp focus. He would then talk of his work as an activist, of how he discovered and fought corruption. He would talk of elected officials, netas, who constantly betrayed those who trusted them.

Sanjay would then tell them why he was different.

He was one of them, a mazdoor: his life was exactly like theirs, so much so that when he went campaigning flanked by other mazdoors, people could not tell who the candidate was. By voting for him, they were voting themselves in.

Furthermore, Sanjay said, his work as an activist meant that he knew how to solve their problems; he was not corrupt and was not supported by any party; his campaign was run entirely by contributions—'*apna paise bhi nahin daal raha hoon*' (I am not putting my own money); he was a fighter, a man who fought for them on the streets and will now fight for them on the inside. Throughout, he assured them, unlike those netas whom they saw once every five years, he would be with them, walk every step with them. And together they would dream and achieve.

'*Ladenge!*' he would call out,

'*Jeetenge!*' they would respond.

We will fight, we will win!

His speeches would suffer interruptions of all sorts: a honking vehicle in the background, a shrieking child, an old man keen to get a word in on the mic, a pair of goats gone astray, a sudden frenzied conversation amongst women in the back. But Sanjay would be unfazed, carefully drawing the attention of the crowd back towards himself—a quick slogan call-and-respond here, a word of admonishment there–his kerchief wiping the sweat off his brow.

Nothing could distract him. He was there to win.

'*Lagta hai ki shooting chal raha hai*,' (It feels like a film shoot!) Sanjay told me over the phone, as he describes the 'camping' heating up.

In what way, I ask.

He tells me of the procession he is part of on the campaign trail. There are long lines of people on foot or bicycles, as also a few slow-moving motorcycles and purring three-wheeled tempos. All these entities–human and machine–sprout appendages: flex banners, flags and pamphlets, all bearing images of Sanjay. Somewhere at the top of the line, a sound-system blares songs and pauses to make grand announcements. People stand by the road or their homes and watch; some are merely intrigued, others want to catch a glimpse of the little man who heads the procession. For his part, Sanjay, at the top of this winding line, walks with folded palms raised above his head. Every now and then, he acknowledges his audience with a winning smile and a nod.

Ye sab, all this, Sanjay tells me, has the feel of a movie set.

I ask if he has ever seen a movie set. He says he hasn't, but *this*–this chaotic procession of men and women and sound and fanfare and curious onlookers–is how he thinks it would feel like to be on one.

(I had once, back in 2015, asked Sanjay if he had ever seen a movie. 'Never in a theatre,' he had said, but then corrected himself. 'Actually, once–I was doing the wiring work for a cinema hall and they projected a few scenes on the big screen just to see if things were okay. I watched.' It is an image I can conjure in my mind's eye with ease: a scrawny Sanjay in a dark and depopulated single-screen cinema, watching agape the magic of moving images.)

Movie set or not, the mazdoors of Kurhani did make it to local and national television screens. In September, on a grey, windy late monsoon day, Mandesri Devi, her white hair visible from beneath her pink and blue dupatta, spoke live to Ashirwad News, a local news channel.[114] With four other mask-wearing women mazdoors flanking her, she stated her case plainly, not faltering once: '*Aath saal se unke saath sangharsh kiya hai, unse laabh mila hai ... Ab tak bahut vidhayak ko humne jitaaye, lekin koi vidhaayak humse taakne nahi aaye ... poore mazdoor milke Sanjay Sahni ko jitaayenge.*' (We have fought alongside Sanjay for eight years and benefited from him ... Thus far, we have elected many MLAs, but no one came back to check on us ... Thus, all the workers have decided to jointly elect Sanjay Sahni.)

Sanjay himself gave a slew of interviews. In each one of them, he cast himself as the voice of the mazdoors, as the one most likely to defeat the incumbent BJP MLA. Some newspapers covered his campaign, but many were reluctant to allocate a lot of space without any payment on his part. It was not like he asked them to cover him. Many newspaper editors called him up on their own and stated their price, usually in the range of Rs 1–2 lakh.

In October, Sanjay's old friend Jean Drèze came visiting. This boosted the campaign's visibility. *Prabhat Khabar*, a leading Hindi newspaper, carried a piece with the question: 'Why is the famous economist Jean Drèze in Muzaffarpur?' A video interview the newspaper carried on their YouTube channel begins with still

[114] Watch her here: https://www.youtube.com/watch?v=Vhlx4HcQXVs.

photographs of Drèze and Sanjay and a thunderous background score more suited for visuals of Kattappa in *Bahubali*. After about thirty seconds of the music and the stills, Drèze appears on screen. Standing on a busy street in Muzaffarpur town, he succinctly makes the case for Sanjay: he notes that the campaign is historic, since it features a candidate who has emerged from the people—one who is not contesting on the back of his wealth, but on the basis of a decade's worth of work. Drèze says that he has seen Sanjay up close and has been witness to his stellar work on the NREGA, rations and pensions, and praises his commitment to furthering the cause of justice and equality.

Around this time, Sanjay also appeared on Sreenivasan Jain's *Reality Check* on NDTV. As one of four panellists discussing the role of returning migrants in shaping the elections, a forceful Sanjay, who spoke in Hindi, told Jain that the migrants had had enough. They wanted change. The BJP and JDU—the parties that comprised the incumbent alliance—would be voted out. While Sanjay spoke, NDTV flashed images of Sanjay and the mazdoors on campaign trail, flags and fists raised, snaking across tiny village lanes in Kurhani.

For the interview, Sanjay donned the blue-and-white chequered shirt that I remembered from the posters. He also wore this shirt in a separate interview with the *Hindustan Times*'s Sunetra Choudhury, an interview with *Prabhat Khabar* and in various images accompanying interviews of him in print-media outlets. I asked Sanjay if this was planned.

He laughed and said it was the only nice shirt he had.

October also saw the arrival of students from across the country. Responding to a call made by Drèze, about twenty of them turned up to help with campaigning. The online news portal *Print* profiled some of them and their reasons for doing so. Here's an excerpt:[115]

> Ankita Aggrawal, a student at the New York University, has come from Delhi to assist Dreze.
>
> 'It's a people's movement, they are leading the campaign of Sahni. We are contributing in some way. I wanted to be a part of a movement which is led by women, so I packed bags and came here to make a change,' said Ankita.
>
> Another volunteer, Chirag, a Graduate in Developmental Politics from London, who works in Ranchi, said: 'He (Sahni) says when you choose to bring a change in the society, you have to first change yourself. I am working in Jharkhand and Sahniji is working in Bihar. We know his work, so even we thought of working to bring a change at our own place.'
>
> Shailja Tandon, who works at the Centre for Social Sciences and Humanities in Delhi, said: 'I want to be part of the transformation which is happening in this Bihar village. It is a crusade against systematic politics. That's why I came here to be a small part of the movement.'
>
> Every day, Dreze, with students and volunteers like Chirag, Ankita and Shailja, travels to different villages with Sahni and several women labourers.

The campaign team on the ground had broadened: from the MW/SPSS loyalists to returning migrants to youth to local social workers, and finally now to students. More students, sitting in their homes in Delhi and Bengaluru and Satna and Patna, volunteered to steer the social-media campaign. Stunning

[115] Shankar Arnimesh and Taran Deol, 'Economist Jean Dreze is campaigning for this electrician-turned-activist contesting Bihar poll', *ThePrint.in*, 1 November 2020, https://theprint.in/india/economist-jean-dreze-is-campaigning-for-this-electrician-turned-activist-contesting-bihar-poll/535038/.

social-media posters were created: Sanjay and women mazdoors straight out of a red-and-white watercolour dream; Sanjay, spade in one hand, the phone in another, clad in a white banian, with a caption in Hindi that translated to: *Sanjay Sahni, not a ruler, but a friend.* The social-media team, working in tandem with the students traversing the villages, rapidly conjured many videos, campaign materials and press releases.

The beating heart of the campaign, however, were the women mazdoors. They had stood by Sanjay from his very first sabhas at NaREGA Chowk in 2012. Rajendran Narayanan, who visited Ratnauli in the final phases of the campaign, wrote about these women—whom he referred to as 'NREGA didis' (which is how they were known locally)—in the *Indian Express*:[116]

> [They] walk each day, some bare feet [sic] and some with kids in arms, raising slogans in support and solidarity. This is despite having no income and little food. NREGA didi Indu Devi's foot came under an autorickshaw recently and Mandeshri fractured her hand a few days ago. When we asked Indu Devi about it, she casually said, 'We have now learned that even we have rights. If we can do so much without being in power, imagine how much more can be done if we have political power'.
>
> Regardless of the outcome of the election, the complex journey from not knowing what their ration entitlements

[116] His piece on how a collective of NREGA activists discovered their political voice is here: Rajendran Narayanan, 'NREGA didis of Kurhani', *The Indian Express*, 4 November 2020, https://indianexpress.com/article/opinion/nrega-didis-of-kurhani-6927389/. In an email to me and a few others, a few days after he returned from Muzaffarpur to Bengaluru, Rajendran wrote of his time among the mazdoors: 'Each day had something inspiring to offer. I just didn't want to leave. It was after a long time that I felt so damn alive and "in the moment".'

are to conceiving that they can have a say in the Legislative Assembly is almost like a fairy tale. The resilience of the NREGA didis presents much hope.

My WhatsApp conversations with Sanjay are strewn with messages like these:

Saran g plz paise ka pata kijiye, printing wala ko dena hai (29 June)

Saran g paise ka kuchh pata chala kya (22 July)

Plz paise ka kuchh kijiyega jaruri hai (27 August)

Jo paise aap bhejne wale the nahi aaya (27 October)

They are all variants on the same theme: urgent requests for money.

Every sustained fight for justice, social or political, requires funds. An election is a particularly expensive fight. An election in India prohibitively so.

Even a campaign machinery as rudimentary as Sanjay's needed financing. Here is a non-exhaustive list of items the campaign incurred expenses on, grouped loosely by broad category of expenditure: pamphlets, posters, flex banners, flags; diesel for tempos and motorcycles, bicycles, masks, a basic sound system; food and chai (and some petty cash) for campaigning volunteers; garlands, vehicles on rent–autos, jeeps, motorcycles–for roadshows, a big speaker; polling agents who help with 'getting out the vote' and monitor counting.

In May 2020, as the campaign strategising began, Sanjay's bank account had fewer than Rs 50,000. The mazdoors who, courtesy the lockdown and then the floods, had seen their savings vanish, could cobble together a few thousand more at best. A campaign would need at least Rs 6 lakh, about ten times as much.

Here is where we came in: a group of Sanjay's supporters, all of whom had worked in the development sector–as activists, academics and professionals–and had been inspired by the amazing MW/SPSS mazdoors. Most of us had spent some time in Ratnauli and had supported the movement for years. We wrote to our friends and family, peers and even sympathetic acquaintances. We set up a strict expenditure accounting system: the mazdoors kept bills for all their expenses during the campaign. Mandesar Ram, ward member, collected all bills, gave each one a unique number and noted expenses in a physical ledger he kept. Photographs of every single bill were then sent to a data-entry team in Patna that entered them all into an excel sheet.

In September, we launched a page on the crowdfunding portal *Our Democracy*.[117] Over the next two months, a grand sum of Rs 10,12,584 was raised on the portal. A total of 227 donors contributed. The highest donor by far was the writer Arundhati Roy. Roy once wrote that '[An]other world is not only possible, she is on her way. On a quiet day, I can hear her breathing.'[118] Perhaps, in the campaign, she heard more than a breath, maybe a whisper or the first line of a new song of hope?

And yet, as men and women have learnt ever since society began employing metal objects in the exchange of goods, *the money was never quite enough*. As election day neared, expenses soared. More feet hit the ground and the roadshows grew extravagant: both Sanjay and his wife Sarita were now

[117] Here's how *OurDemocracy* defines itself: 'OurDemocracy is a technology platform that is aiming to create a level-playing field for political candidates. The platform is non-partisan and offers technology solutions that encourage candidates from all political parties in India to raise funds for their projects and election campaigns and enroll volunteers.'

[118] Arundhati Roy, *Capitalism: A Ghost Story*, Haymarket Books, Chicago, 2014.

campaigning, standing atop jeeps and entwined in marigold garlands. Women mazdoors piled in on autos and paraded the streets of villages near and far. Substantial sums were spent on a phone campaign that blasted a pre-recorded message from Sanjay to thousands of voters.

Jean Drèze—still camping in Muzaffarpur—circulated an appeal for funds on 22 October. After briefly describing Sanjay and his story, the appeal read:

> This is a low-budget campaign funded by individual donations. Money is short for everything, from printing to transport and even phone calls. Please consider contributing ... Whatever you may be able to spare will be highly appreciated—every rupee counts.

In the final two weeks before polling day, the other main parties—the BJP and the RJD—swung into action. Their machinery was better-greased, their propaganda blitz was blinding, their roadshows boasted booming mega-speakers and vehicles galore: where Sanjay had tempos, they had trucks and SUVs. Their volunteers waltzed across the landscape and offered promises, but more importantly, money. 'A five-hundred-rupee note folded into every pamphlet distributed to households,' Sanjay told me.

The way the big parties approached their campaigns has been standard fare in the (few) elections I have had the privilege to see unfold from close quarters. It is a formula Mahendra Singh Dhoni applied to great effect while chasing totals in limited-over cricket games. Like Dhoni, the parties bide their time, waiting and then waiting some more. And then, just as the end nears and all appears lost, they whir into action, blowing away their opponents in a blistering display of power and fury.

The two main parties spent money in crores, much of it in black. This is an open secret. Even the former Indian prime minister Atal Bihari Vajpayee is supposed to have said: 'Indian politicians start their legislative careers with a lie—the false spending returns they submit.'[119]

Sanjay's campaign, which ran on well-wishers' and mazdoors' contributions, cost Rs 15 lakhs and was a rare exception to the Vajpayee dictum. The amount spent on his campaign was not even 50 per cent of the legally permitted expenditures in the election.

On 6 November, the day before polling, I received this message from Sanjay: *Plz polijent ke liye kuchh aur paise ka kuchh kijiye*. It was a request to raise money to pay 'polling agents'.

The campaign had ended, but its thirst for money remained.

I had seen the end coming even before it began.

Three types of persons start any election campaign with massive disadvantages: those who are poor, or without any party support, or are first-timers. Sanjay ticked all three boxes.

We had run some polls over the phone, of a sample of politically active respondents in Kurhani. The samples were biased and collecting sensitive data over the phone was always going to be tricky. The polls were, therefore, distinctly unscientific and, at best, indicative. But, given the DIY nature of the entire campaign, it was all we could do.

In July, only about 30 per cent of our polling respondents had even heard of Sanjay. That number had risen slowly, to

[119] As the article notes, he was in opposition then: Sunanda K. Datta Ray, 'Do politicians declare their real wealth?', *Rediff.com*, 1 May 2004, https://www.rediff.com/money/2004/may/01guest2.htm.

touch 50 per cent by late September. The share of persons who said they would vote for Sanjay hovered around 10–15 per cent. We knew, even then, that we needed double that number for the campaign to be competitive.

Sanjay was up against a force stronger than those survey numbers. This was the sheer weight of history. For decades, activists across the country had contested and lost. Medha Patkar. Dayamani Barla. Venkat Reddy. Irom Sharmila. These were all stellar human beings who had placed their lives in the service of their people; they had achieved much, transforming the lives of so many. They had run clean campaigns on principled platforms. Yet, the people chose to reward them with damning electoral losses.

In several conversations over many months, Sanjay betrayed nothing but a confidence bordering on the cavalier. When we told him the polling numbers—which he invariably took a great interest in—he would listen and then question our sample: have you reached enough women? Are you able to speak with mazdoors or are only the rich and the elite answering your phone calls? He was right to ask those questions, of course. Our sample was biased and in exactly the directions he anticipated; but could our estimates be *so* off?

On other occasions, he would point to the upward trend in his popularity across multiple rounds of polling. People were beginning to know him, he claimed. The campaign was working. He could feel it in his daily door-to-door jan-sampark expeditions. Come November, he would win.

It was all very fierce, grand and fantastic. It was a delusion to behold.

Why did I spend so much time on a campaign that was the metaphorical equivalent of a roadshow veering into a ditch in slow motion?

First, and this is the least important reason, I believed that the academic in me—the one that studied political economy for a living—would benefit from seeing something like this play out from the inside. The campaign encompassed several of my core academic interests: understanding ways to amplify the voices of the marginalised, the interlinkages between social movements and electoral politics, deciphering voter preferences over politicians and policies.

Second, as someone invested in Bihar, this campaign was an experiment both worth undertaking and supporting. It was a shoestring, bottom-up, mazdoor-and-women-driven campaign. In its audacity, it represented not a break from, but a continuity in, Bihar's political evolution. The rise of Lalu Yadav and Nitish Kumar had propped up the powerful backwards and challenged the hegemony of the entrenched upper-caste elites of Bihar. The long arc of democracy bent towards social justice, creating space for broader representation. This campaign presented the next step in that evolution: it was driven by a coalition of extremely backward castes and Mahadalits, featuring women and landless workers.

Third, the campaign's significance transcended the boundaries of Bihar, as evidenced by the considerable coverage it got in the national media. Indian electoral democracy has, for a while, been a bastion of the rich and the privileged. In an era where politics is usually practised by those endowed with a famous surname or substantial wealth, Sanjay's campaign held out a promise for the type of politics Indian democracy could use to redeem itself. What's more, a partially respectable showing, perhaps 10,000 votes for Sanjay, could lay the platform for greater enthusiasm for such candidates. The bigger successes would follow. The campaign, therefore, served—and stood out as—a symbol.

Fourth, and most importantly, because Sanjay was a friend. Over the years, we have spent many a happy day in each other's company, visiting each other's homes, exchanging ideas and jokes, and talking late into the nights. We come from vastly different worlds: mine spoke Kannada, his spoke Vajjika; my childhood home had three bedrooms, tiled roofs, cement walls, and was filled with books and cricket bats and modern electronic gadgets; his house in Ratnauli, to this day, has a door so low that we stoop to enter, a single tiny room, mud walls, mud flooring and an open cook-stove.[120] Yet, we get along like a house on fire. It is this deep friendship, alongside his—and the women mazdoors'—inextinguishable flame that inspires me to support and embrace MW's many radical ideas.

Fifth, and finally, because everyone hopes. The survey-based odds, the caste calculations, the weight of history, all of these may have been stacked against Sanjay, but I still thought that there was a small—perhaps vanishing—chance that the campaign may produce an upset and Sanjay would emerge victorious. Or, as Jean Drèze called it in an email to me: *a good surprise*. Hope alone may not have been enough, but as I grew more and more

---

[120] While his own house is bare of electrical appliances, Sanjay's acquaintance with these gadgets, courtesy his former life as an electrician, is an intimate one. Once, he had come to visit me in Delhi and we were talking late into the night. At one point, I got up to heat my tea in the microwave. Sanjay followed. We were discussing the movement, his future, the role of women and so on. Suddenly, he paused and, pointing to the microwave, said: 'There is a plate at the base of this thing ...' and proceeded to give me a detailed explanation of how it worked. It came out of nowhere and caught me by surprise. It was at that moment that I became fully aware of the vast gap he had bridged when he made the leap from electrician to activist.

invested in the campaign, hope kept me going, like a cup of hot chai at the end of a long day.

It was the day after polling day, 8 November.

'Did you do a phone survey to see how people voted?' Sanjay asked over the phone. His voice was husky, fragments of sentence-ending words seemed to disappear. All that speech-making and sloganeering had taken a toll on his voice.

I said we did not have the money. Moreover, what use will it be? The results would be out in three days.

He sounded quieter than usual. This was, I realised, not only because of his weak voice.

'*Kya hua*,' I asked. Was everything okay?

A pause. Then: 'I don't know.'

For the first time in months, I recognised an emotion that I had presumed missing in Sanjay's ouvre: *doubt*.

Our views about the campaign were finally converging: over the past week, I had become slightly more hopeful because of a flawed poll we had run that showed Sanjay doing quite well. On the other hand, Sanjay, having got first-hand reports of actual votes polled, had begun to question his chances.

I told Sanjay not to worry. That, whatever the result, he should be proud of the campaign the mazdoors had fashioned. I also told him that, even if he loses, he would put up a respectable showing.

'10,000–25,000 votes,' I told Apurva, my wife, as counting was about to begin. This amounted to 5–12.5 per cent of all votes polled. I was confident: the mazdoors had run a spectacular, spirited campaign. The people, especially other mazdoors and the poor, had responded. Our friends who had travelled to Kurhani–Drèze, Rajendran–were optimistic. Even our latest phone surveys had shown positive trends.

10 a.m. IST is almost midnight in the United States. By a little past midnight, I had refreshed the election commission's results page enough times to realise that I was wrong: the sparkling campaign was buried under a landslide of votes that went to the BJP and RJD candidates.

This was, it dawned on us, not a contest, but a massacre.

Sanjay had won just over 2.5 per cent of the votes. In all, he had polled less than 5,000 votes and lost his deposit.

The top two candidates had polled around 40 per cent each. The RJD candidate, Anil Kumar Sahani, had won. The incumbent BJP MLA, Kedar Prasad Gupta, with whom Sanjay thought he was in a 'straight fight', lost by 1,000 votes, but even he had polled a whopping 70,000 more votes than Sanjay. The third-placed candidate, a certain Ram Babu Singh, whom Sanjay had not mentioned once in all our conversations, won more than twice as many votes as fourth-placed Sanjay.

I worried for Sanjay and the mazdoors, who had never once doubted themselves. Once the results were confirmed, I called Sanjay, but his phone was unreachable. I sent him a message praising the incredible campaign he and the mazdoors had fashioned. The next morning, he responded, in Devanagari script: 'जी बिल्कुल सरण जी, कैंपिंग में आप सभी का पूरा सहयोग मिला। बहुत धन्यवाद।' (Of course, Saran-ji–you have all helped a great deal with the campaign. Thank you!)

I spoke to him two days later. He told me he was okay, but the mazdoors were distraught. Some had come to the office and wept. He was not fully sure why he had lost—he would take stock over the next few days. We spoke of other things: of his impending travel to Ranchi to be with his family, of the upcoming Chhat festivities, of the fog that was beginning to descend in the mornings. It was a wonderfully normal conversation.

A day later, he sent a WhatsApp message with a PDF which listed the results from the four polling booths in Ratnauli. Sanjay was number one, polling the maximum votes, in all of them. 'The mazdoors of Ratnauli,' he wrote in a text that followed, 'have given a stinging reply to the BJP and RJD candidates.'

The very next day, he shared a photograph featuring a group of men seated on a yellow tarpaulin sheet and him in the centre. In the back, one could spot Mandesri Devi and a few other women mazdoors. This was all from a recent meeting of migrant workers that he had organised in Ratnauli.

A week later, Sanjay and a few of his closest supporters—those who, like me, had helped with various aspects of the campaign—had a call to discuss the elections and the aftermath. We had all been deeply invested in the campaign.

Sanjay spoke of the work MW and SPSS would continue to do in the coming months. Then, almost casually, he said he had just launched a brand-new collective exclusively for migrant workers. It was called PMG. He repeated himself: *Pee–Aem–Jee.* It was short for 'Pravaasi Mazdoor Group' (Migrant Workers Group). The issues migrant workers faced, he told us, were both severe and immediate: a collective dedicated to their cause was the need of the hour.

A new collective, a fresh agenda, another leap for the stars.

An inextinguishable flame.

Sanjay had moved on. It was time we did too.

9

And That's the End of That

In late 2013, I was applying to PhD programmes abroad. This warranted a visit to Delhi University, to acquire official transcripts of my grades. After spending a few hours with an old bully—the administrative offices of my alma mater—I found myself on the road that wound back to the Metro station. I was on a battery-rickshaw: an autorickshaw–cycle-rickshaw mutant, purring three-wheelers that were motorised and yet not quite, and almost wholly absent from my days there as a student.

The rickshaw-wallah was smartly dressed. Well-oiled hair, neatly side-partitioned, a crisp white shirt under a brown half-sweater. He invited me to share his seat with him. We got talking and I asked him where he was from.

Old haunts flitted past me: the Institute of Economic Growth on my right, Kirori Mal College on my left.

He was from Bihar.

I perked up. A recent love.

Where in Bihar?

Somewhere close to Bhagalpur, he explained.

What district?

Banka.

He asked me if I was from Bihar too. I said I was not. I had worked there though, I told him. With the government. On the NREGA.

NaREGA, he said knowingly.

I was pleased. It was like someone else knew of a book I loved.

'How long were you in Bihar?' he asked.

A year-and-a-half, I said. I then rattled off the districts I had been to in a breathless whirl–AurangabadBegusaraiBhojpur SamasitpurMadhubaniNawadaNalandaSiwanSamastipurAraria KatiharPatnaKaimurRohtas–as though doing this would convey somehow how strongly I felt for his homeland.

'Have you gone to school?' I asked.

'Yes.'

'How far did you study?'

'Till class IX.'

'Why did you stop?'

'My brother died and my parents were getting old ... My brother worked here, in Delhi. Some of his old contacts remained. So I got work here.'

'What did your brother do?'

'He was a truck-driver'

'Oh.'

(In Calcutta the previous year, I had met a former truck-driver from Lakhisarai, also in Bihar. He was in his late thirties and said one couldn't drive a truck beyond a certain age: the life can get very lonely, the hours are crazy, the time away from family takes its toll. 'But the money', he told me, 'the money makes it hard to leave.')

'My brother had an accident,' the rickshaw-wallah explained. 'He was driving and his truck broke down. So he parked on one side of the road and went to sleep, as was his wont, on top.

It was dark and late in the night. It was not far from here. In Jahangirpuri. When he was sleeping, another truck came at full speed and rammed into my brother's. He flew off the top and fell into the drain. And that was the end of that.'

I am reminded of another winter morning, thousands of kilometres away. We are driving through rural Bihar, looking to interview the mukhiyas of villages. After being misdirected a few times–a frustratingly common occurrence–we arrive at the mukhiya's house. His wife tells us he has gone to the fields. We thank her and drive towards the fields, which is when we notice a commotion in the distance. Our driver says it is not safe to go any further and insists we take a detour. I am curious, I want to know *what* it is that has happened. We hail a passer-by.

'What's going on?' our driver asks.

'Muddar.'

'What?' I ask. It's a word I haven't come across and I've picked up a fair amount of the local dialect.

'*Muddar ho gaya*,' the driver enunciates every word.

I feel like a five-year-old. Then it dawns on me: murder.

This is what happened: A woman was burnt to death because she eloped with a man from another caste. Her charred body lay in the fields.

And that was the end of that.

We are now going past Miranda House, the traffic thickens.

The rickshaw-wallah was still chatting away: 'We got six lakh in compensation. From the truck company. We have filed a case in the Tees Hazari court. We should get three lakh more. Even the other two families must get.'

'Other two?' I asked.

'Oh yes, there were two labourers who died too. You know, those chaps who used to travel in these trucks with my brother.'

It was remarkable how easily he was speaking of all this. Things happen, people die, we get money, life moves on. It reminded me of what Amartya Sen said once when he came to give a talk in Patna, that the present is a really tiny sliver in the expanse of time, that a moment is history before you can even comprehend it. It is over, gone, ended. And the next one is here.

'The truck-malik's nephew is our lawyer,' he explained. 'He's very confident of getting us the money. He got us six lakhs in six months—we can get another three lakh by the end of the year, hopefully.'

I nodded my head, Rs 9 lakh was relatively decent compensation. Farmers who commit suicide in Maharashtra got Rs 5 lakh. Bomb-blast victims in Patna the previous week got a Rs 1 lakh each and an asthi-kalash yatra, an ash-immersion procession.

We were now nearly at the metro. The rickshaw-wallah showed me how nimble his battery-rickshaw was, as we navigated a space that could barely hold two of me.

'Thank you,' I said as I paid him.

Many in Bihar, more men than women, live dual lives: one in the city, the other in the village. This book is squarely about the villages—and village politics in particular—but the story of Bihar is as much about those in whom it resides as it is about those who reside in it. This type of dual existence is doubly precarious: migrants exist in a room of windows, peering into everyone's worlds, but not quite having one of their own.

This book is filled with migrants: it begins with the people's movement in Araria—whose frontrunners, Ashish Ranjan and

Kamayani Swami[121] are both returning migrants–and centres around the likes of Sanjay Sahni and Mandesar Ram, both of whom sought their livelihoods away from home for long stints.

When these protagonists returned, they confronted a social order simultaneously similar to and dramatically unlike the worlds they had left behind. Similar because, beneath the veneer of anonymity the city affords, lay the old hierarchies of caste, class and creed. For the migrant worker, the best ways to navigate the city is to rely on village-based networks. When the migrant from Ratnauli was stuck during the pandemic, the first call came to Sanjay Sahni.

Yet, the village is different, because power manifests differently. The state is more central to the lives of the poor. In villages, the marriage of caste and class politics has produced mukhiyas in whom power is concentrated. Despite incomplete devolution of powers to local governments–or perhaps precisely because of that–the mukhiyas function as little autocrats, their feudal writ running large over their constituents.

This book documents five ways to challenge–and distribute–the power of the mukhiyas.

First, through reservations. The battle for political reservations in Bihar was long and hard-won. The normative grounds for reservations are clear: Dalits are greatly under-represented in the political arena. Anyone who believes that democracies should be representative in the true sense of the term should have few quibbles with reservations. But there are empirical grounds too, as our research has shown: reservations help

[121] Ashish was trained as an engineer and Kamayani studied development and social change at the Tata Institute of Social Sciences in Mumbai. Subsequently, they both lived in the United States for a few years before returning to Bihar to dedicate their lives to running JJSS in the districts of Araria and Katihar in east Bihar.

Dalits—socially, economically, politically—with negligible costs to non-Dalits.

Second, through decentralisation. Ward members are elected representatives, but often only in name: empowering them—financially, administratively—could help contain the writ of the mukhiyas. Additionally, wards are often caste homogenous: hence, Dalits and other oppressed castes have managed to elect one of their own as ward members even in the absence of reservation. Thus, ward members are more representative of the population they are elected from and less likely to be encumbered by the trappings of electoral politics.

Third, building transparency and monitoring measures that allow citizens to question the stories governments fabricate. If the NREGA law did not mandate transparency—rules that ensured mukhiyas uploaded the wage rolls online—Sanjay Sahni would have remained an electrician in Janakpuri. A well-functioning grievance redressal system is another check on the state's tall tales. Kamal Manjhi's mukhiya had refused to release funds. The grievance redressal mechanism ensured that the wrong was righted.

Fourth, through social movements. Collective action—especially in a society as hierarchical and fractured as India—is a hard and complex process. But, when it works, it could transform lives. SPSS and MW have been a source of great hope, succour, purpose and joy for thousands of mazdoors in Muzaffarpur and beyond. The remarkable nature of the movement is that it is entirely home-grown. The electrician whose madness sparked this movement was born there.[122]

---

122 Bihar has also experimented in a big way with setting up extremely local women's self-help groups (SHGs) under the Bihar Rural Livelihoods Project (BRLP), better known as JEEViKA. Over 1 crore women are part of JEEViKa's network, attending regular local meetings, giving out and receiving small loans, expanding networks and learning about and participating in

Another forum for collective bargaining of citizens with those in power is the gram and ward sabhas: these institutions are works in progress, but could form the bedrock of building a more equal and just society.

Finally, through voting and elections. 'One person, one vote' is a potent equalising force. While electoral democracy may not be an unvarnished blessing, it is undeniable that those representing us—corrupt as they may seem—are less and less like the elites who once governed us. This is progress. Elections reinforce divisions[123] and spur majoritarianism, it is true. These are, however, small costs to pay for what electoral democracy has allowed us: to throw out those who have not served us and to allow us to dream of new possibilities.

One such possibility would be to make it easier to contest in electoral politics. I asked Mandesar Ram if he would stand again. He answered: 'Bilkul' (Of course!). Mandesar was talking of the upcoming ward elections, which, owing to the pandemic, now stands indefinitely postponed. But why could he—or someone like him—not contest the mukhiya elections? 'Ratnauli's mukhiya's post is not reserved for us,' he explained. In Bihar, as perhaps in other places, it is commonly assumed that a post not reserved is the exclusive domain of the upper

---

government programmes. JEEViKA has been transformational in affecting gender relations in rural Bihar. In a 2015 paper, Paromita Sanyal and co-authors argue that JEEViKA: '(1) is capable of inducing large-scale cultural change that leads to greater gender equality, and that (2) this is not simply a matter of making behavioral "nudges" at the individual level, but is akin to creating a mini-social movement within the village that challenges traditional structures of power and patriarchy.'

123 While I was still in Delhi University, where we had elections every year, I was often struck by how deep the animosities ran, and yet, how quickly they disappeared. Come September, the month of voting, the Biharis and the Jats would be at daggers. By December, it would all be forgotten, only to be rekindled once more in July, in preparation for a new term.

caste men.[124] Thus, any upward mobility in most panchayats among, say, the Dalits (since only a sixth of the panchayats is reserved) is scuttled. This must change.

That being said, despite Sanjay Sahni's own electoral ambitions suffering a blow, the larger people's movement is keen on fielding candidates in the upcoming panchayat elections, for the posts of ward member, mukhiya and sarpanch. 'We have a list of 150 candidates from different villages,' Sanjay tells me. Surely, one would assume, accessing political power would augur well for the movement. Sanjay and the mazdoors think it would, but they are also somewhat cautious. Sometimes, becoming a member of local government changes loyalties: outsiders on the inside behave like insiders. Power corrupts. A few members are lost to the movement, though several remain and some flit in and out. This is the way of village politics.[125]

If the ladder from ward member to mukhiya is steep, especially for those from marginalised groups, the one from mukhiya to MLA is non-existent, and not only for the disadvantaged.[126] An MLA constituency contains thirty-four panchayats (on average): in an ideal world, a locally important political actor,

[124] Ratnauli's mukhiya's position is currently reserved for women, but, often, men get around that concern by having someone from their own family contest the elections.

[125] In principle, mukhiyas and mazdoors affiliated with movements are opposing forces. For someone to assume both roles would be to live a contradiction. This is a question I have debated at some length with Sanjay and the mazdoors, with none of us having any clear answers.

[126] Mukhiyas do become presidents of panchayat samitis, a block-level body, or the zilla parishad, its district-level equivalent, but these positions are not the same as becoming an MLA: first, these posts are indirectly elected, for example all the mukhiyas in a block elect one among themselves to be the panchayat samiti president; second, they command a fraction of the political power the MLA does. Moreover, the path from these posts to becoming an MLA is also fraught and difficult.

who has burnished her credentials serving the needy in village government (and higher panchayati raj institutions), should be able to aspire to contesting and winning the MLA elections. This rarely, if ever, happens. Mandesar may become mukhiya, but he laughs when I suggest he think about MLA elections at some point in the future. In principle, a good system should have a way of sending up talent from the bottom. If this were to happen, it would both increase the quality of elected members in local government and prevent higher-level politics from becoming the exclusive domain of the rich and the elite, as it so often is in India.

This book began as, and remains, an endeavour of modest ambition: as a record of my time in Bihar.[127] I noted down my field experiences because I feared I would forget. The big things are permanently lodged in the crevices of my brain—the honking, the corruption, the immense potential for change. But what of the little things? Take for instance, the *smell* of government offices: a curious mix of brittle files and old furniture, tinged with urine when there's a toilet around the corner.

Here is the other thing about Bihar and hazy memories—rural Bihar, even more than rural India—seems to be afflicted by a general fogginess about the past: the windshield of memory is always misted up. What's more, rather than try and fix it, everyone winks at it. This is most easily manifested in a general

---

127 This section and the one that follows draw from a piece I wrote in the *Economic and Political Weekly*. See: M.R. Sharan, 'Remembering and Forgetting in Bihar', *Economic and Political Weekly*, Vol. 53, No. 39, 2018, https://epw.in/journal/2018/39/postscript/remembering-and-forgetting-bihar.html.

sort of genial impreciseness. For instance, Sanjay Sahni lives in Ratnauli. Pavittar Paswan—fellow-villager and comrade, balding and warm—lives in Natrauli. I once asked Sanjay about the two names. He said he had never noticed the difference between the two words until I pointed it out. Later, I asked Paswan-ji and his response was even more baffling: he could not tell them apart even *after* I had pointed it out. This is not an isolated case. The board for the town of Narsanda in Biharsharif reads 'Lasanda'.

This extends easily to language itself. Hindi conflates yesterday and tomorrow. Paswan-ji takes this one step further. He conflates next and previous (a not-uncommon occurrence among Hindi-speakers in these parts), leading to unhinging conversations.

When did your father die?

Next year.

Surveying is a nightmare anywhere, and ideally, data collected from respondents needs to be cross-checked, back-checked, double and triple-checked. But Bihar is in a league of its own. You can spend hours with members of a household, only to be presented with an entire gamut of responses that are both contradictory and circular.

Sample this half-remembered conversation from somewhere in Rohtas.

A little context: I am sitting on a charpoy in front of a thatched hut that borders a ditch of some sort. The ditch is deep, so one needs a tiny wooden trapezesque bridge to get across to the hut. We are trying to track households off online records. This means that we are contending with layers and layers of imprecision, intentional and otherwise. There is the actual event, the unofficial paper-based record of the event and the official record entered online; then there is the memory of the event, the foggy memory of the world in general and the vague notion of undemarcated time.

'Have you *ever* worked on the NREGS? On tree-plantation, earth-work?'

'Yes, we planted trees.'

'Where?'

'Somewhere.'

'Somewhere where?'

'Somewhere east.'

'East? Where east?'

'East is where east is.'

'Do you remember anything else?'

'We worked next to a canal, somewhere east.'

'What canal?'

'It was next to *that*.'

'*That*?'

'Yes.'

[Uh oh.]

'When did you work?'

'One-two-five years ago.'

'One, two or five?'

'Two.'

'Not one?'

'One.'

[Pause, deep breath.]

'So this was in 2011?'

'Sometime after the rains, maybe a couple of years ago.'

[Noted. New line of attack.]

'It says here you worked on the road construction that happened near Sukh Ram's field?'

'Sukh Ram has a field?'

'Sukh Ram has a field.'

'Oh yes, now I remember, he does.'

'So?'

'So he has a field.'

'Yes, I just told you that. Did you help construct that road?'

'What road?'

'The one next to Sukh Ram's field?'

'Eh?'

'In May this year, apparently you helped construct a road next to Sukh Ram's field.'

'Which Sukh Ram?'

'But I just thought you told me you knew of his field.'

'What's his father's name?'

'It doesn't say here–but have you worked on *any* road construction?'

'Yes.'

'When?'

'About one–two years ago.'

'Oh, but it says here you worked in May this year.'

'Maybe May.'

'But you just said *two years ago*!'

'Maybe it was not two years ago.'

[Pause, gulp down water, breathe, start anew.]

Impreciseness affects us all, but that is why we record. And why we revisit.

Time, for most, is linear. The future is ahead, the past behind, the present is here. Time is also increasingly fine and graded: in our world, the vast Pangaea of the past is chopped into tiny grain-sized events. The word 'now' is largely used to convey this hour, minute or second. Indeed, the present seems to get more anorexic with every passing generation.

In rural Bihar, for many of the poorest, time is linearly cyclical.

Imagine life to be divided into three broad truck-journeys: childhood, adulthood and old age. In each of these journeys, we view life from the driver's seat, having a full view of the many different things that life has to throw at us. On the other hand, rural Bihar has a tyre-side view of life, coasting along in cycles, from day to night and night to day. Time, like the truck, surges ahead, but *life*, from the perspective of the wheel, moves in familiar patterns. Yesterday is like tomorrow is like today. Or, past *is* present *is* future. Of course, there are changes every now and then—a flood here, a puncture there—but, on the whole, within each of these journeys, life is remarkably repetitive. Money matters, assets vary, respect accumulates: but graded time is inconsequential.

What is the *need* then for precise memory, when history has fused with the present?

The future is stripped of any semblance of certainty. The pandemic, which rages and wanes like the tides, has already kept me away from Bihar for over a year.

I do intend to be there this summer. I will return to Patna, eat sattu paranthas at Rakesh-ji's guest house, chat with the flat-nosed anda-wallah by A.N. College; he has a degree in Psychology. I will visit Chinmaya's sister, Shruti, who housed and fed me, and whose children entertained me, on multiple visits during the PhD. I will pay a visit to the ADRI offices, if only to chat up Mantu-ji, the pot-bellied security guard from Begusarai. At some point in the day, I will go see Chanchal, whose brand-new company and office I have only glimpsed in photographs.

I will then travel to Muzaffarpur, perhaps catch an '80s Raj Kiran movie if I take the bus; I will deboard at Turki and mount a shared-auto—ten in the back seat, five facing five, knees jutting and kissing—to Mahant Maniyari. A six-year-old will stare at my alienesque headphones. I will smile, perhaps even show her how they sound.

My first glimpse of Maniyari chowk will probably be the red brick of the Sanskrit College against ominous monsoon clouds. I will then turn rightwards, now perhaps on foot, and navigate narrow dusty lanes—comprising the odd cow, motorcycles and bicycles, houses forever unfinished, open drains with black sludge, the dazzling smile of an old mazdoor friend—to emerge at a clearing. This is Ram Babu's house, behind which is the SPSS office. Dukha-ji, Ram Babu's father, his hair growing whiter with every passing year, will be on his charpoy, resting his bad leg. When he sees me, he will call out and smile his half-toothed smile.

And behind, by the office, a group of conversing women—Mandesri Devi's shrill, joyous voice ringing in the fresh rain-laden air—and gentle Mandesar Ram. When they see me, they will raise their fists in unison and smile. *Zindabad.*

And somewhere among them, perhaps instructing someone over the phone or checking government records on his laptop screen or joking with some women mazdoors, will be Sanjay Sahni. We will perhaps share a hug, exchange pleasantries. I will mock his expanding belly, he will ignore my small talk.

Then, in his deathly officious tone, he will begin: 'Saran-ji...'

Index

D

I

J

K

L

M

U

V

W

Y

Z

Acknowledgements

Last Among Equals *is one long thank-you note to Sanjay Sahni and the mazdoors of Muzaffarpur.*

This book on Bihar was conceived in Washington DC in the summer of 2020. All around us, a deadly virus raged, the air was heavy and still, the roads soundless. I had recently attended my PhD graduation ceremony, via Zoom. Kanishka Gupta, my agent, congratulated me on Facebook and asked me if I was still writing: 'What about non-fiction ... based on your PhD?' And so, I began poring over nearly ten years' worth of field notes, fed on a steady diet of delicious home-cooked Tamil food—courtesy our friends Siddharth Hari and Anusha Ramakrishnan, who kindly let us stay at their place for many weeks—and late-night four-way Ludo games.

This book benefited from excellent research assistance from two brilliant and hard-working scholars: Sheikh Safwan did background research for the initial chapters; Shreya Jaipuria untiringly dug up, digested and commented on every single important case in the reservation jurisprudence and also walked me patiently through the intricacies of the law. Many fine researchers assisted me during my PhD, from which parts of this book draws upon. I am grateful to Chanchal Kumar Singh, Suraj Kumar, Rakesh Kumar, Neha Verma, Bhanu Shikha, Varun Kapoor, Manasi Rao and Meghna Yadav. My PhD advisors—

Gautam Rao, Abhijit Banerjee, Emily Breza and Asim Khwaja—brought much-need direction and rigour to my research on Bihar.

I am also grateful to a host of incredible people who helped with discussions, comments, read-throughs of chapters and other miscellaneous inputs that have all gone a long way in shaping this book: Krupa Ge, Aditya Sarkar, Kalyani Raghunathan, Roshan Kishore, Dipa Sinha, A. Santhosh Mathew, Abhishek Anicca (whose poetry and knowledge of Bhojpuri came in handy), Venu Aggarwal, Nandini Gupta, Anindita Adhikari, Ravi Bamezai, Rita Misri Bamezai, Anand Mamidipudi, Mamidipudi Achyutha, Vikram Srinivas, Siddharth George, Samvartha 'Sahil' and Siddharth Chauhan. Tanay Nagarjuna, my half-Bihari nephew (though he will never admit it in public), is all of fifteen and read most of this book, sending me pithy summaries and effusive praise. He moved from reading this book to the unabridged version of Plato's *Republic*, which makes me wonder if he'd take a crack at decoding the Indus Valley inscriptions next. Arvind Subramanian's 'EXCELLENT' verdict on the first chapter of this book boosted my confidence early on. He is unselfish with his time, ungrudging in his praise and unbelievably supportive.

Several members of my family influenced this book profoundly. My parents, Sudha Vidyasagar (Amma) and M.S. Vidyasagar (Appa), read every single word I wrote, engaged deeply with the material and offered comments over many months' worth of phone calls. They kept close track of the progress of this book, facilitating my writing by simply being there. This is very much in line with how they've always been: for instance, in 2013, in rainy June, Appa and Amma travelled across the length of the country to come to Ratnauli with me, spending time with Sanjay and the mazdoors. My brother Swaroop—he and his wife Krupa are long-time remote supporters of the Muzaffarpur mazdoors—read the chapters, brought greater clarity to my ideas, sourced all sorts of court cases-related documents, introduced me to Shreya and was the supervisor for all things legal in this book. My aunt Shantha Sinha sent me long emails with pointed comments, often drawing upon insights from her own experiences as a celebrated activist and political scientist, all of which vastly improved my writing. My cousin Prabha Mohan sent passionate voice messages with terrific suggestions.

My first brush with Bihar was in 2007, when I went to attend a wedding of a relative-by-marriage. Himanshu and Dipa Sinha (who are both economists and also family), with whom I travelled that first time, introduced me to Bihar and have, over the past decade-and-a-half, been very generous with their time, patience and insights. Much of how I view Bihar is shaped by many years of interactions with Chinmaya Kumar, who has also been my long-standing collaborator on a slew of research papers. Chinmaya, who grew up in Sitamarhi, is a fine scholar and a greater friend: his family, especially his parents and his sister Shruti, have housed me over the years, in Patna and Sutihara.

I am extremely grateful to the institutions that have supported my many years of research in Bihar, foremost among which is the Asian Development Research Institute (ADRI). ADRI is a singular institution, a shining pillar in the research and policy space of Bihar. I do not know of another research institute anywhere in India that has so thoroughly shaped government policy. The late Shaibal Gupta, who was always ready to share the wealth of his experience and knowledge, was a pioneer: I wish he could have seen this book. At ADRI, I am particularly grateful to Suryakant-ji, Sunita-ji and the ever-cheerful Mantu-ji. The IDFC Institute was another great source of support over the years. Niranjan Rajadhyaksha's wise counsel and wonderful company is something I always look forward to. The Center for Global Development here in DC gave me a liberal post-doctoral fellowship and a very free hand: much of that time was spent plotting and then writing this book. The University of Maryland's Agricultural and Natural Resource Economics department, where I am employed currently, has a fantastic supportive and collaborative environment, making work on this book stress-free.

A gamut of bureaucrats and a clutch of elected officials across Panchayats in Bihar have helped me better understand village politics. There are far too many to name, but I am particularly grateful to Sanjiv Kumar (State Election Commission) and Raghuvansh Kumar Sinha (Panchayati Raj), both of whom greatly improved my understanding of how reservations were implemented.

Jean Drèze has played many roles in shaping this book: as a character who makes appearances, a source of perpetual personal awe, a purveyor of laconic wisdom, a friend of Sanjay Sahni's. Nikhil Dey also shows up often in these pages: listening and learning from him—often via Sanjay—over the past many years has given me much food for thought. In the past year, I have been fortunate to work alongside Vijayendra (Biju) Rao. Over the next few decades, if I have even a quarter of his passion for local democracy, a fifth of his wealth of knowledge and a sixth of the body of work he has produced, I would consider my work-life a success.

In addition to everyone above, I owe much to all those who have come before me, the scores of researchers, writers, journalists, scholars, chroniclers of Bihar and beyond, who have helped build my understanding of Bihar. Many of them are strewn across these pages, sometimes lurking in the footnotes. I am grateful to them. Any mistakes in this book, needless to say, are mine alone.

Ajitha G.S.'s faith in my writing only rivals my mother's: she is a superb editor and an even better person. Working with her is a dream. I cannot think of a better literary agent than Kanishka Gupta: his counsel at different points have made this experience near seamless.

Both in the years leading up to and during the writing of this book, Apurva Bamezai, my wife, to whom this book is dedicated, suffered through many—too many?—Bihar-related words and ideas, numbers and figures, debates and arguments. Her suggestions on this book were outstanding. We first bonded when we both lived in Patna, making her, in a deep sense, Bihar's greatest gift to me. The book dedication is entirely from the heart, even while it also serves as a bribe—for this Bihar journey is very far from finished and she will invariably bear the brunt of everything that is to come!